Alabama RICH IN FLAVOR

by

Katherine Helms

Cover design and book layout by Asher Graphics

Manufactured in China

Pennylane Press
in association with McClanahan Publishing House, Inc.

All book order correspondence should be addressed to:

Pennylane Press
1801 Pennylane SE
Decatur, AL 35601

256-466-8192

alrichflavor@charter.net

Dedication

For my husband Vance, without him, I would have never discovered my love for cooking. He has endured many creative food experiments. When they have failed, his support has given me the confidence to keep trying.

Introduction

When my husband and I moved to Decatur, Alabama, one of my earliest impressions was the hospitality and social graces of the community. Whether it be a church picnic or lunch with friends, food was a focal point. When I would inquire about a particular dish, many times the recipe would be one adapted from an old family recipe. It is clear that Alabama cooks take pride in the history of the food they serve as well as the taste and presentation.

As a mother of young children, I find it difficult to prepare elaborate meals; therefore, I have incorporated my own attempts at simplifying recipes while maintaining the flavor. Most ingredients can be found in your local grocery store.

Whether you cheer "Roll Tide" or "War Eagle," football is king in Alabama. In celebrating this phenomenon, I have included a section on tailgating. Many of these recipes can be transported or grilled at the stadium or served in front of the TV.

While collecting recipes for this book, I was reminded of the diversity of the state— from the hills and valleys of North Alabama all the way to the beaches of the southern Gulf. Every region supplies its own gift to the palate. Fresh tomatoes and peaches, pecans and peanuts, sweet potatoes and shrimp all serve to make *Alabama Rich in Flavor*.

Contents

Acknowledgements

I want to thank my dear friends and family for contributing some of their favorite recipes to this book. I especially want to thank Cindy Moore for her help in gathering recipes from other parts of the state and for her many personal recipes. Also, Peggy Collins and the Alabama Bureau of Tourism and Travel were generous in their donation of images that are seen on the cover and within the book. Thanks also to the following photographers and sources; Kevin Glackmeyer, Lee Sentell, Karim Shamsi-Basha, Gulf Coast Convention and Visitors Bureau, Grey Brennan, Chilton County Chamber of Commerce, Perdido Vineyards and Rousso's Seafood Restaurant.

Appetizers

FIRST IMPRESSIONS

My oldest daughter has many food allergies, so I often make hummus as it meets many of her nutritional needs. Ironically, my other two children love hummus even more. As babies they would eat it straight without chips. It would make quite a mess. Once while my mother was babysitting, Mimi, my youngest daughter, asked for hummus. When my mother said she didn't have any and she didn't know how to make it, my 21-month-old daughter said, "Nana, you need chick-peas." Many 21-year-olds do not know what goes in hummus but it is definitely a staple around our house, even the babies can make it!

Hearty Hummus Dip

16-ounce can garbanzo beans (chick-peas), drained,
reserving liquid
1 tablespoon lemon juice
1/4 cup ground almonds
1/2 teaspoon salt
1/2 teaspoon pepper
1 garlic clove, minced
1 tablespoon olive oil
2 teaspoons cumin

Combine the garbanzo beans, 1/2 tablespoon of the reserved liquid and lemon juice until smooth. Add the almonds, salt, pepper, garlic, olive oil and cumin; mix well. Serve with tortilla chips.

Serves 4

Cheesy Bacon Ball

8 ounces shredded sharp Cheddar cheese,
at room temperature
8 ounces mayonnaise
1 bunch green onions, chopped
1 pound crispy bacon, drained and crumbled
Parsley, chopped

Combine the cheese and mayonnaise in a large bowl; mix well. Add the onions and bacon; mix well. Cover and chill. Remove the cheese mixture from the refrigerator and form into a large ball. Roll in the chopped parsley before serving. Serve with butter crackers.

Serves 20

Anne's Easy Cheese Dip

Two 8-ounce packages cream cheese, softened
2.5-ounce packet hot chili seasoning
2 tablespoons salsa

Combine the cream cheese, chili seasoning and salsa until smooth. Serve with wheat crackers.

Serves 20

Layered Bean Dip

14-ounce can black beans, rinsed and drained
1 cup sour cream
2 avocados, peeled
2 tablespoons lemon juice
1/4 cup chopped onion
Salt
1 1/2 cups salsa
1 cup Cheddar cheese

Purée the black beans; spread in the bottom of a serving dish. Layer the sour cream over the beans. Purée the avocados, lemon juice and onion until smooth; salt to taste. Spread the mixture over the sour cream. Layer the salsa and cheese. Serve with tortilla chips.

My Birthday Club is a group of women who meet each month at one of our homes. My mother's generation played Bridge, and I know many women who play Bunko; however, I really enjoy this group who gather simply to enjoy good food and great friends. Anne Price brought this dip to one of our get-togethers. I couldn't believe how scrumptious and simple it was to make.

Alabama
RICH IN FLAVOR

This makes a beautiful appetizer for any holiday gathering.

Telete's Pesto-Cheese Torta

2 sticks unsalted butter
Four 8-ounce packages cream cheese, divided
6 ounces grated Parmesan cheese
10-ounce jar traditional basil pesto
10-ounce jar sun-dried tomato pesto

Combine the butter and 2 of the packages of cream cheese in a food processor; blend until smooth. Add the Parmesan cheese; process until well blended. Spread the cream cheese mixture into a 6-cup mold. Combine the remaining cream cheese and basil pesto; process until smooth. Spread over the white cream cheese layer. Cover the mold and refrigerate for several hours. Remove from the mold and top with the tomato pesto before serving. Serve with crackers.

Quick Artichoke Dip

6-ounce jar artichoke hearts, drained and chopped
1 cup mayonnaise
1 1/2 cups mozzarella cheese
4.5-ounce can chopped green chiles

Combine all of the ingredients. Pour the mixture into a baking dish and bake at 350 degrees for 20 minutes or until bubbly and the cheese begins to brown. Serve with crackers.

Miss Alabama's Dill-icious Party Spread

8-ounce package cream cheese
6-ounce jar artichoke hearts, drained and chopped
I cup mayonnaise
I cup Parmesan cheese
I tomato, chopped
I teaspoon dill
I cup grated sharp Cheddar cheese

Combine the cream cheese, artichoke hearts, mayonnaise, Parmesan cheese, tomato and dill. Top with the grated Cheddar cheese. Place the mixture in a greased baking dish. Bake at 350 degrees for 30 minutes. Serve with crackers.

Miss Alabama 1991, Wendy McDougal, gave me this recipe. The dill and tomato add an interesting twist to your basic artichoke dip.

Creamy Mexican Dip

8-ounce package cream cheese, softened
8-ounce can Shoe Peg corn
10-ounce can tomatoes and green chiles

Combine all of the ingredients. Pour the mixture into a baking dish. Bake at 350 degrees for 20 minutes. Serve with corn chips.

Sisters are an interesting breed. Even when we are grown, we seem to still share so much. My friend Jonica got this recipe from her younger sister, Jen. Though Jen lives in Birmingham and Jonica in Decatur, they talk daily and it's no surprise they exchange recipes.

Spinach and Artichoke Dip

Two 10-ounce boxes frozen spinach, thawed
1 tablespoon minced garlic
2 tablespoons minced onion
1/4 cup butter
1/4 cup all-purpose flour
1 pint heavy cream
1/4 cup chicken stock
2 teaspoons lemon juice
1/2 teaspoon hot sauce
1/2 teaspoon salt
2/3 cup grated Romano cheese
1/4 cup sour cream
12-ounce jar artichoke hearts,
drained and coarsely chopped
1/2 cup shredded Monterey Jack cheese

Drain the spinach and squeeze to remove as much of the liquid as possible. Sauté the garlic and onion in the butter over a medium heat. Stir in the flour and cook for 1 minute. Slowly whisk in the cream and chicken stock; cook until it boils. Stir in the lemon juice, hot sauce, salt and Romano cheese. Remove from the heat and allow to cool for 5 minutes. Stir in the sour cream, dry spinach and artichoke hearts. Sprinkle the Monterey Jack evenly over the top. Microwave to melt cheese and serve with tortilla chips.

Serves 8

Vidalia Onion Dip

3 large Vidalia onions, chopped
3 tablespoons butter
8 ounces shredded sharp Cheddar cheese
1 cup mayonnaise
1 garlic clove, minced
1 teaspoon hot sauce

Sauté the onions in the butter until tender.   Combine
the cheese, mayonnaise, garlic and hot sauce; beat until
blended.   Add the onions; mix well.   Spread the mixture
into a 2-quart shallow baking dish. Bake at 375 degrees
for about 20 minutes or until golden.   Serve with
corn chips.

Swiss Bacon Dip

8-ounce package cream cheese, softened
1/2 cup mayonnaise
1 cup grated Swiss cheese
2 tablespoons chopped green onion
1 pound bacon, cooked and crumbled
1 cup crushed butter crackers

Combine the cream cheese, mayonnaise, cheese, onion
and bacon in a medium bowl. Pour the mixture into a
7 x 11-inch coated glass baking dish. Sprinkle the crackers
on top. Bake at 350 degrees for 15 to 20 minutes. Serve
hot with crackers.

Kickin' Crab Dip

1 small onion, chopped
1/2 green pepper, chopped
1 garlic clove, minced
3 tablespoons butter
6 ounces sharp Cheddar cheese
3 ounces cream cheese
4 tablespoons ketchup
1 teaspoon hot sauce
1 tablespoon Worcestershire sauce
1 tablespoon sherry
6.5-ounce can crab meat

Sauté the onion, pepper and garlic in the butter. Add the cheese, cream cheese, ketchup, hot sauce, Worcestershire sauce, sherry and crab meat. Serve with corn chips or crackers.

Gulf Shrimp Dip

A trip to Gulf Shores is not complete without sampling fresh seafood. My favorite is the shrimp. This recipe can be made with frozen shrimp, but you can imagine how wonderful it is with the fresh catch of the day.

Two 8-ounce packages cream cheese, softened
1 tablespoon mayonnaise
3 tablespoons cocktail sauce
1 onion, grated
1/4 teaspoon salt
1/2 pound shrimp, finely chopped
1/4 teaspoon Tabasco sauce
1/4 teaspoon Worcestershire sauce

Combine all of the ingredients in a mixer. Let stand for several hours. Serve with chips.

Cheese Stuffed Mushrooms

1 pound medium-size mushrooms
1/4 cup finely-chopped green onions
1 garlic clove, minced
1/4 cup butter
1/2 cup dry bread crumbs
1/4 cup Parmesan cheese
2 tablespoons parsley
1/2 teaspoon salt
1/2 teaspoon dried basil
1/4 teaspoon pepper

Remove the stems from the mushrooms and finely chop the stems. Sauté the mushroom stems, onions and garlic in the butter for 5 minutes or until tender. Remove from the heat and stir in the bread crumbs, Parmesan cheese, parsley, salt, basil and pepper. Fill the mushroom caps with the stuffing mixture. Place the mushrooms, filled side up, on a coated baking dish. Bake at 350 degrees for 15 minutes. Serve hot.

Alabama
RICH IN FLAVOR

Green Pepper Jelly

**6 large green peppers,
cut into pieces with seeds removed
1 jalapeño pepper
1 1/2 cups vinegar
1/2 teaspoon salt
6 cups sugar
1 bottle liquid pectin
Green food coloring**

**Place the peppers in a blender container. Add the vinegar
and process until liquefied. Pour the mixture into a
saucepan. Add the salt and sugar. Bring to a full boil and
boil for 1 minute. Remove from the heat and stir in the
pectin. Let stand for 5 minutes. Stir in several drops of
the green food coloring. Pour into sterilized jars and seal.
Serve with cream cheese and crackers.**

Makes 4 1/2 pints

I got married in December and we tried to keep with a Christmas motif. My mother felt pepper jelly would be a perfect addition to the holiday fare. Though pepper jelly was not on the hotel's list of catered food, she convinced them to allow her to fix her recipe and guests were served pepper jelly at the reception. The caterers learned, as I learned long ago, there is no stopping my mother once her mind is set.

Cranberry Salsa

12-ounce package cranberries
4 tablespoons chopped fresh cilantro
1/3 cup lime juice
1/2 teaspoon salt
1/4 teaspoon pepper
1 jalapeño pepper, minced
1 tablespoon grated onion
1/2 cup sugar

Blanche the cranberries long enough for them to split open; drain. Pulse the cranberries in a blender container. Add the remaining ingredients. Chill and serve with cream cheese and crackers.

Peachy Sweet Guacamole

2 medium-size ripe peaches, pitted and chopped
3 green onions, chopped
1 avocado, peeled, pitted and chopped
1 small jalapeño pepper, stemmed,
seeded and finely chopped
1 garlic clove, minced
3 tablespoons chopped fresh cilantro
3 tablespoons orange juice
1/4 teaspoon salt

Combine all of the ingredients in a medium bowl. Serve with tortilla chips or cinnamon graham crackers.

Makes 1 1/2 cups

Avocado and Black Bean Salsa

1 avocado, diced
5 ounces frozen corn, thawed
14-ounce can black beans, drained and rinsed
2 1/2 plum tomatoes, diced
1/4 cup chopped white onion
4 tablespoons olive oil
2 tablespoons lemon juice
1 tablespoon red wine vinegar

Combine the avocado, corn, beans, tomatoes and onion. Combine the olive oil, lemon juice and red wine vinegar in a bottle; shake. Drizzle over the other ingredients and let sit for an hour. Serve with tortilla chips.

Beverages

REFINED REFRESHMENTS

Morning Tropical Fruit Blend

15.5-ounce can cream of coconut
46-ounce can pineapple juice
12-ounce can frozen orange juice, thawed
7 1/2 cups water

Set the cream of coconut in hot water before opening to avoid congealing. Combine all of the ingredients in a large container; stir well.   Serve chilled.

Makes 1 gallon

Tart and Tasty Fruit Punch

6 pints cranberry juice cocktail
1 1/2 quarts orange juice
1 1/2 cups water
2 1/2 cups strained lemon juice
3 cups pineapple juice
3 cups sugar

Combine all of the ingredients; chill.

Serves 50

Wassail

1 gallon apple cider
2 sticks cinnamon
1/2 cup honey
3 whole cloves
1 1/2 cups orange juice
1 1/2 cups lemonade
1/2 teaspoon nutmeg
2 teaspoons lemon rind

Heat the cider, cinnamon sticks, honey and cloves in a large saucepan. Bring to a boil over a medium heat; simmer, covered, for 5 minutes. Add the orange juice, lemonade, nutmeg and lemon rind. Simmer for 10 minutes.

Serves 40

Fabulous Fruit Tea

7 regular-size tea bags
1 1/2 cups water
1/4 cup sugar
12-ounce can frozen orange juice concentrate, thawed
12-ounce can frozen lemonade concentrate, thawed

Brew the tea and water. Remove the tea bags and add the sugar; stir until dissolved. Pour the mixture into a 1/2 gallon pitcher. Add the juices. Fill to the top with water. Refrigerate until ready to serve.

Rarely do I attend a casual social gathering or planning meeting when this tea is not served.

You may substitute vanilla ice cream or chocolate vanilla swirl for a more subtle chocolate flavor.

Coffee Punch

1 gallon chocolate ice cream
1 pint whipped topping
1 gallon strong sweetened coffee, chilled
1/8 teaspoon salt
1 cup rum

Scoop the ice cream into a punch bowl. Add the whipped topping, coffee, salt and rum; stir gently.

Serves 40

Steamy Percolator Punch

9 cups unsweetened pineapple juice
9 cups cranberry juice
4 1/2 cups water
1 cup brown sugar
4 1/2 teaspoons whole cloves
4 sticks cinnamon
1/4 teaspoon salt

Place the juices and water in the bottom of a 30-cup percolator. Place the sugar, spices and salt in the top basket. Plug in the percolator and allow to perk.

Serves 35

Baby Shower Banana Punch

4 cups sugar
6 cups water
12-ounce can frozen orange juice
6-ounce can frozen lemonade
6 mashed bananas
6 cups pineapple juice
10-ounce package frozen strawberries
1 quart ginger ale

Bring the sugar and water to a boil in a saucepan; cool completely. Add the frozen orange juice, lemonade and 2 containers full of water. Stir in the bananas, pineapple juice and frozen strawberries. Freeze in 2 gallon ice cream buckets. Remove from freezer 4 hours before serving. Add the ginger ale; stir. This punch should be slushy when served.

Serves 50

Cori's Party Punch

64-ounces cranapple juice
64-ounces white grape juice
2-liter bottle ginger ale
16-ounce bag frozen cherries

Any frozen fruit will do as it serves to keep the punch cool. The cherries add a rich color.

Pour the juices and ginger ale together into a punch bowl. Add the cherries when ready to serve.

Montgomery Mint Tea

3 cups boiling water
4 regular-size tea bags
12 fresh mint sprigs
1 cup sugar
1/4 cup lemon juice
1 cup orange juice
5 cups water
Fresh mint
Orange slices

Pour the boiling water over the tea bags and mint in a pitcher. Cover and steep for 5 minutes. Remove the tea bags and mint, squeezing gently. Stir in the sugar, juices and water. Serve over ice. Garnish with the fresh mint and orange slices.

Tea for 50

1 1/2 cups hot water
4 cups sugar
6 cups pineapple juice
4 cups orange juice
1 cup lemon juice
1/2 gallon weak tea
2-liter bottle ginger ale
Fresh mint

Dissolve the sugar in the water; cool. Add the juices to the tea. Pour into a pitcher and add the ginger ale before serving. Serve over ice in tall glasses. Garnish with the fresh mint.

Breakfast/Brunch

MORNING MASTERPIECES

Sweet and Sassy Apple Dumplings

Two 10-ounce cans refrigerated crescent rolls
3 Granny Smith apples, peeled and chopped
2 sticks butter, melted
1 cup sugar
1 teaspoon cinnamon
10-ounce can Mountain Dew

Place two crescent rolls together to make a rectangle; repeat until all rolls are used. Cover each rectangle with the apples; fold up like a package. Place, seam side down, in a coated 9 x 13-inch baking dish. Combine the butter, sugar and cinnamon; pour over the rolls. Pour the Mountain Dew over the top. Bake at 350 degrees for 35 minutes.

Serves 8

Bob Dishman's Easy Apple Cheese Bake

Two 20-ounce cans sliced apples, drained
2 sticks butter, softened
2 cups sugar
I pound processed cheese, cubed
I 1/2 cups all-purpose flour

Place the apples in a coated 9 x 13-inch baking dish.
Cream the butter and sugar. Add the cheese; blend well.
Beat in the flour gradually. Smooth the cheese mixture on
top of the apples. Bake at 350 degrees for 20 minutes.

Serves 20

Sour Cream Coffee Cake

18.25-ounce box yellow cake mix
1/4 cup firm butter
1 cup brown sugar, packed
1 cup chopped pecans
3 eggs
1 1/2 cups sour cream

Measure 2/3 cup of the dry cake mix and pour into a small bowl. Cut in the butter. Add the brown sugar and pecans; set aside for topping. Beat the eggs lightly with a fork in a large bowl; stir in the sour cream. Blend in the remaining cake mix. The batter will be thick and slightly lumpy. Pour 1/2 of the batter into a coated and floured 9 x 13-inch baking dish. Sprinkle half the brown sugar topping over the batter. Spoon and gently spread the remaining batter into the pan; top with the remaining brown sugar topping. Bake at 350 degrees for 35 to 40 minutes.

Trish's Cranberry Cream Cheese Pull Aparts

5-ounce package dried cranberries
20 frozen white dinner rolls, thawed but still cold
1/4 cup butter, melted
1 cup sugar, divided
6 ounces cream cheese, softened
3 tablespoons orange juice
1 tablespoon grated orange rind
1 tablespoon grated lemon rind
1 cup confectioners' sugar
5 teaspoons lemon juice

Press 5 to 6 cranberries into each thawed roll. Place the rolls in a coated 9 x 13-inch glass baking dish. Combine the butter, 1/2 cup of the sugar, cream cheese and orange juice; blend well. Pour over the rolls. Cover with plastic wrap and let rise about 1 1/2 hours in a warm stove or until double in size. Combine the remaining 1/2 cup of sugar, rinds and any remaining cranberries. Sprinkle this mixture over the risen rolls. Bake immediately at 350 degrees for 25 to 30 minutes or until the rolls are done in the center. Combine the confectioners' sugar and lemon juice; drizzle over the rolls.

RICH IN FLAVOR

Fruit Pizza

Two 20-ounce rolls sugar cookie dough
10 ounces vanilla chips
8-ounce package cream cheese, softened
2 cups sliced strawberries
I cup blueberries or I cup sliced kiwi

Cut the dough into slices and press into a coated pizza pan. Bake at 350 degrees until lightly brown on top. Melt the vanilla chips and cream cheese together in the microwave; stir until smooth. Spread the cream cheese mixture over the crust after the crust has cooled. Arrange the fruit on top immediately before serving.

If planning to serve later, you can keep the fruit from browning by combining 1/4 cup sugar and 1/2 tablespoon cornstarch; stir in 1/4 cup pineapple juice and 1/4 teaspoon lemon juice. Cook over a medium heat, stirring constantly until thick. Pour the juice mixture over the arranged fruit.

Doughnuts from Centre

8 cups all-purpose flour, divided
2 packages active dry yeast
1/2 cup water
2 cups milk
1 cup butter
2 teaspoons salt
1 cup sugar
4 eggs, beaten
Grated rind and juice of 1 lemon
1/2 teaspoon nutmeg
Vegetable oil

Combine 4 cups of the flour and yeast. Heat the water, milk, butter, salt and sugar in a saucepan until butter is almost melted; stirring constantly. Pour the milk mixture into the flour; add the eggs. Mix using an electric mixer on low speed adding 3 cups of the flour, lemon rind, lemon juice and nutmeg gradually. Beat for 3 minutes on a high speed. Knead the dough adding the remaining flour. Form into 1 ball. Place in a coated bowl and turn to coat all sides. Cover and let rise for 1 1/2 hours. Punch down and fold onto a lightly-floured surface. Divide the dough into 2 balls; roll each ball to 1/2–inch thickness. Cut with a floured doughnut cutter. Cover and let rise for 1 hour. Heat oil to 375 degrees. Fry the doughnuts for 1 minute. Turn and fry for another minute. Cover with glaze.

Glaze

2 cups confectioners' sugar
1/2 teaspoon vanilla extract
Milk

Combine the confectioners' sugar, vanilla extract and enough of the milk to make a drizzle.

Raspberry Cream Cheese Coffee Cake

21/4 cups all-purpose flour
1 cup sugar, divided
3/4 cup margarine
1/2 teaspoon baking powder
1/4 teaspoon salt
1/2 teaspoon baking soda
3/4 cup sour cream
1 teaspoon almond extract
2 eggs, divided
8 ounces cream cheese, softened
1/2 cup raspberry preserves
1/2 cup sliced almonds

Combine the flour and 3/4 cup of the sugar. Cut in the margarine; mix well. Reserve 1 cup of the mixture; set aside. Add the baking powder, salt, baking soda, sour cream, almond extract and 1 of the eggs; blend well. Spread over the bottom and sides of a coated 9 x 13-inch baking dish. Combine the cream cheese, remaining sugar and egg; blend well. Pour the cream cheese mixture over the crust. Spoon preserves evenly over the cream cheese mixture. Combine the reserved mixture and almonds; pour over the preserves. Bake at 350 degrees for 45 to 50 minutes. Let cool for 15 minutes.

Serves 16

You may substitute 1/2 cup of any fruit preserves or fruit pie filling.

Stacked Huevos Enchiladas

2 pounds top round
1 packet tenderizing marinade
1 packet Southwest marinade
24 corn tortillas
3 cups Colby/Jack cheese
1 pound mushrooms, sliced
10-ounce can green chile enchilada sauce
16 eggs
1 yellow or red pepper, sliced
1 green pepper, sliced

Marinate the beef in both of the marinades in the refrigerator overnight. Broil or grill the beef until medium. Slice the beef into thin strips. Fry the tortillas until crisp. Layer a tortilla with beef, cheese and mushrooms. Cover with enchilada sauce; repeat. Complete each stack with a third tortilla. Bake at 350 degrees for 15 minutes. Fry eggs and place two eggs atop each tortilla stack. Sauté the peppers for garnish.

Serves 8

Standard Sausage Quiche

12 ounces bulk pork sausage
9-inch pie crust, unbaked
8 ounces shredded mozzarella cheese
8 eggs, beaten
1 1/2 cups milk
1 teaspoon salt
1/2 teaspoon pepper

Brown the sausage and spread in the pie crust. Combine the cheese, eggs, milk, salt and pepper. Pour the egg mixture over the sausage. Bake at 375 degrees for 25 to 30 minutes.

Never Enough Sausage Balls

These sausage balls have such a subtle flavor that it is easy to eat many. They go quickly and there are rarely any leftovers.

1 1/2 cups baking mix
3 cups shredded Cheddar cheese
1/2 cup finely-chopped onion
1/2 cup finely-chopped celery
1/2 teaspoon garlic powder
2 pounds pork sausage, uncooked

Combine all of the ingredients in a bowl. Roll the mixture into small balls. Place the balls on a coated metal baking sheet with a lip. Bake at 375 degrees for 15 minutes or until brown.

Bridget's Spicy Sausage Casserole

1 1/2 pounds pork sausage
16 ounces spicy cheese spread
6 eggs, beaten
Two 10-ounce cans refrigerated crescent rolls

Brown the sausage. Melt the cheese spread in the microwave until smooth. Add the eggs to the melted cheese; blend well. Pour the mixture into the sausage. Layer one can of the crescent rolls on the bottom of a coated 9 x 13-inch baking dish. Flatten to cover the entire dish. Pour the sausage mixture over the crescent rolls. Place the second can of crescent rolls on the top. Bake, covered, at 350 degrees for 25 minutes. Remove the cover and bake for 5 additional minutes or until the top layer is lightly brown.

Serves 20

My friend Bridget said that when she got married, she didn't know how to cook so every meal was some concoction of refrigerated crescent rolls or Hungry Jack Biscuits and some sort of meat. Though she's moved on to cooking more complicated fare, this recipe is one of her best.

Breakfast Sausage Bread

Two 1-pound loaves frozen white bread dough, thawed
1/2 pound mild pork sausage
1/2 pound hot pork sausage
1 cup sliced mushrooms
1/2 cup chopped onion
3 eggs, divided
3 cups mozzarella cheese
1 teaspoon dried basil
1 teaspoon dried parsley
1 teaspoon dried rosemary
1 teaspoon garlic powder

Allow the dough to rise until nearly doubled. Brown the sausage; drain. Add the mushrooms and onion; cook until tender. Set the sausage mixture aside to cool. Beat 1 of the eggs; set aside. Add the remaining eggs, cheese and seasoning to the sausage mixture. Roll each loaf of dough into a 12 x 16-inch rectangle. Spread 1/2 of the sausage mixture on each loaf leaving 1-inch of dough around the edges. Roll jelly roll style, starting at the narrow end; seal edges. Place on a coated baking sheet. Bake at 350 degrees for 25 minutes. Remove from the oven and brush the top with the reserved egg. Bake an additional 5 to 10 minutes or until golden brown. Slice and serve warm.

Recipe can be made using dough for Refrigerator Rolls on page 45.

Breads

PALATABLE PLEASURES

Crispy Butter Rolls

10-count package refrigerated biscuits
1/2 cup Parmesan cheese
1/2 cup crisp rice cereal
1 stick butter, melted

Cut each biscuit in half. Combine the cheese and cereal in a shallow bowl. Dip each biscuit half in the butter, then in the cheese mixture. Place on an uncoated baking sheet. Bake at 400 degrees until lightly browned.

Makes 20 biscuits

Bleu Cheese Rolls

One package pre-baked dinner rolls in
aluminum foil pan
1/4 cup bleu cheese
1/2 stick butter

Though I have seen recipes similar to this one, my friend, Bridget, made the process easier by using the rolls in the foil pan.

Poke deep holes in the top of the dinner rolls using a fork. Melt the bleu cheese and butter in the microwave. Pour over the rolls; cover and refrigerate for 2 hours or freeze until ready to serve. Bake according to package directions.

Broccoli Cheese Cornbread

8 1/2-ounce box corn bread/muffin mix
4 eggs
1 onion, minced
1 stick butter
10 ounces frozen broccoli, thawed and drained
2 cups shredded Cheddar cheese

Combine all of the ingredients. Pour into a coated 9 x 13-inch baking dish.   Bake at 350 degrees for 30 to 40 minutes.

This is a great way to get your kids to eat broccoli.

Sweet Potato Cornbread

2 cups self-rising cornmeal
1/4 teaspoon salt
1 tablespoon self-rising flour
1 egg
1 cup buttermilk
2 medium-size sweet potatoes, peeled and cubed
1 1/2 tablespoon oil

Combine the cornmeal, salt, flour, egg and buttermilk with a fork; blend well. Boil the potatoes until tender. Drain and mash. Add the potatoes to the cornmeal mixture. Coat a cast iron skillet; add the mixture. Bake at 350 degrees for 20 minutes or until brown on top.

Beer Bread

3 cups self-rising flour
1 teaspoon salt
3 tablespoons sugar
12-ounces beer

Combine all of the ingredients. Pour into a coated 9-inch loaf pan. Bake at 350 degrees for 1 hour.

Granny's Dilly Bread

My friend Cindy took her Granny's Dilly Bread recipe and adapted it by adding rapid rise yeast to make the process quicker.

2 packages rapid-rise yeast
1/2 tablespoon sugar
1/2 tablespoon salt
1 tablespoon dillweed
1 1/2 cups oats
4 cups all-purpose flour, divided
1 cup whole wheat flour
2 cups warm water
1/2 cup shortening or bacon grease
1/2 cup chopped onion

Combine the yeast, sugar, salt, dill, oats, 3 cups of the all-purpose flour and whole wheat flour. Combine the warm water and shortening; add the onion. Add to the flour mixture. Knead until smooth and elastic adding the remaining flour as needed. Place in 2 coated loaf pans and bake at 425 degrees for 1 hour or until brown on top.

Makes 2 loaves

Chocolate Lover's Moist Muffins

18.25 ounce box devil's food cake mix
39-ounce can pumpkin
1 cup chocolate chips

Combine all of the ingredients. Pour into muffin tins. Bake at 350 degrees for 12 to 15 minutes.

Makes 12 muffins

The batter will be very thick and will not be smooth. They are moist and have a rich chocolate flavor though the texture is rough. For a low-fat alternative, leave out the chocolate chips.

"More Please" Cheese Bread

1 cup unsalted butter, softened
8 ounces cream cheese, softened
1 teaspoon salt
1 teaspoon thyme
2 1/4 cups unbleached all-purpose flour, divided
4 cups Colby/Jack cheese
2 eggs
4.5-ounce can green chiles

Process the butter, cream cheese, salt and thyme in a food processor. Add 2 cups of the flour and process until a ball forms. Wrap the mixture in wax paper and refrigerate for 1 hour. Pat the dough using floured fingers to 1/4-inch thickness on a coated 12 x 16-inch baking sheet. Bake at 375 degrees for 20 minutes. Combine the cheese, eggs, 1/4 cup flour and green chiles. Pour the mixture evenly over the crust and return to the oven for 20 minutes. Let cool and cut into squares.

Poppy Seed Bread

3 cups all-purpose flour
1 1/2 teaspoons salt
3 1/4 cups sugar, divided
1 1/4 cups oil
2 teaspoons almond extract, divided
2 teaspoons vanilla extract, divided
1 1/2 tablespoons poppy seeds
1 1/2 teaspoons baking powder
1 1/2 cups milk
3 eggs, beaten
1/4 cup orange juice
1 tablespoon butter
1/2 teaspoon lemon extract

Combine the flour, salt, 2 1/2 cups of the sugar, oil,
1 1/2 teaspoons of the almond extract, 1 1/2 teaspoons
of the vanilla extract, poppy seeds, baking powder, milk
and eggs. Pour into 2 coated loaf pans. Bake at 350
degrees for 1 hour. Remove from the oven and loosen the
loaves. Cool for 10 minutes. Combine the orange juice,
butter, remaining almond and vanilla extracts, lemon
extract and remaining sugar. Poke holes in the bread.
Pour glaze over the loaves while warm.

Strawberry Bread

3 cups all-purpose flour
1 cup sugar
1 tablespoon cinnamon
1 teaspoon baking soda
1 teaspoon salt
3 eggs, beaten
1 1/4 cups oil
Two 10-ounce packages frozen strawberries,
thawed and drained

Coat the 2 loaf pans lining the bottoms with aluminum foil. Combine flour, sugar, cinnamon, baking soda and salt in a large bowl. Make a well in the center of the mixture and pour in the eggs and oil; stir well. Stir in the strawberries gently. Bake at 350 degrees for 1 hour. Cool in the pans for 15 minutes. Loosen from the side of the pan using a knife. Turn out and cool completely before slicing.

Welcome Home Sweet Bread

Three 10-ounce cans refrigerated biscuits
1/2 cup sugar
1/2 teaspoon cinnamon
1 cup brown sugar
1 stick butter, melted

Cut each biscuit into quarters. Place the biscuits in a resealable plastic bag. Add the sugar and cinnamon. Place the coated dough in a coated bundt or tube pan. Combine the brown sugar and butter; pour over the biscuits. Bake at 350 degrees for 35 to 40 minutes.

Cranberry-Orange Bread

The first four ingredients mixed in the food processor also make an excellent relish if served alone. However, it is important to always chop the oranges first as they will take longer, then add the cranberries.

2 oranges, unpeeled, quartered and seeded
3 cups cranberries
2 cups sugar
1 cup pecans
4 cups all-purpose flour
3 tablespoons baking powder
2 teaspoons salt
1 teaspoon baking soda
1/2 cup shortening
2 eggs
Orange juice

Pulse the oranges with peel in a food processor until coarsely chopped. Add the cranberries, sugar and pecans; pulse until just chopped, not pulverized. Combine the flour, baking powder, salt, baking soda and shortening in a large bowl. Add the eggs to the orange mixture. Pour into the flour; blend well. Add enough orange juice to thin, if the mixture is too thick. Pour the batter into coated loaf pans. Bake at 375 degrees for 1 hour. Bake 20 minutes if making muffins.

Refrigerator Rolls

I cup water
1/2 cup butter
1/2 cup shortening
3/4 cup sugar
1 1/2 teaspoon salt
2 packages dry yeast
I cup warm water
2 eggs, beaten
6 cups all-purpose flour

Bring the water to a boil in a saucepan. Add the butter and shortening; stir until melted. Add the sugar and salt. Set aside to cool to room temperature. Dissolve the yeast in the warm water; add the butter mixture and eggs to the yeast. Add the flour; blend well. Cover and refrigerate overnight. Turn the dough out onto a floured surface. Roll to desired thickness; cut and shape. Allow to rise for 2 hours on a coated baking sheet. Bake at 400 degrees for 12 minutes. Only bake as many as you need, the dough will keep in the refrigerator for several days.

There are plenty of uses for this dough. The dough is not too elastic and is easy to work with when cold. The following recipes use this dough.

Cinnamon Rolls

1/2 recipe Refrigerator Rolls
1 1/2 sticks butter, divided
2 cups sugar
2 tablespoons cinnamon
Pecans, crushed
Raisins
1 cup confectioners' sugar
2 teaspoons milk
1 teaspoon vanilla extract

Roll the Refrigerator Roll dough to a 20 x 16-inch rectangle. Soften 1 stick of the butter and spread over the dough. Combine the sugar and cinnamon; sprinkle over the butter. Add the pecans and raisins if desired. Roll from the short side and seal the ends. Cut at desired width and put into a coated pan; let rise for 2 hours. Bake at 375 degrees for 25 minutes. Combine the remaining butter, confectioners' sugar, milk and vanilla extract for icing. Add more milk to thin the icing if needed. Ice the rolls while warm.

Orange Rolls

1/2 recipe Refrigerator Rolls
1 stick butter, softened
16 ounces confectioners' sugar
1/4 teaspoon salt
3 tablespoons frozen orange juice concentrate, thawed
1 orange rind, coarsely grated

Roll the Refrigerator Roll dough out to a 20 x 16-inch rectangle. Combine the butter, sugar, salt, orange juice, and rind. Spread 3/4 of the mixture over the dough. Roll up jelly roll style. Cut to desired width and allow to rise in a coated pan for 2 hours. Bake at 375 degrees for 25 minutes. Ice with the remaining mixture, adding extra orange juice to thin the icing.

Almond Rolls

1/2 recipe Refrigerator Rolls
Two 8-ounce packages cream cheese, softened
1/8 teaspoon salt
1 egg
3/4 cup sugar
3 teaspoons almond extract, divided
1/4 cup butter
1 cup confectioners' sugar
2 teaspoons milk
1/2 cup slivered almonds

Roll the Refrigerator Roll dough out to a 20 x 16-inch rectangle. Combine the cream cheese, salt, egg, sugar and 2 teaspoons of the almond extract. Spread the mixture over the dough. Roll up jelly roll style. Cut to desired width and allow to rise in a coated pan for 2 hours. Bake at 375 degrees for 25 minutes. Combine the butter, confectioners' sugar, milk and remaining almond extract to make icing. Drizzle the icing over the rolls and sprinkle with the almonds.

Soups/Salads

SUMPTOUS STARTER

Beverly's Cold Cucumber Soup

1 large onion, sliced
1/4 cup butter
1 large potato, peeled and cubed
Two 14.5-ounce cans chicken broth
4 large cucumbers, peeled, seeded and chopped
1/2 teaspoon dill
1/2 teaspoon salt
1/2 teaspoon white pepper
1 cup sour cream
1 tablespoon apple cider vinegar

Sauté the onion in the butter. Place the onion, potato, broth, cucumbers and seasonings in a pot; cook for 15 minutes or until the potatoes are done. Allow to cool. Purée in a blender container. Add the sour cream and vinegar. Chill until ready to serve.

Chicken Tarragon Soup

1 garlic clove, minced
1 stick butter
1/2 cup all-purpose flour
4 cups half-and-half
Three 14-ounce cans chicken broth
1 teaspoon tarragon
1 pound sliced fresh mushrooms
3 cups cubed cooked chicken
Salt
Pepper

Sauté the garlic in the butter. Add the flour; whisk until smooth. Pour in the half-and-half and chicken broth. Season with the tarragon; add the mushrooms and chicken. Cook for 10 minutes or until mushrooms are tender. Season with the salt and pepper.

Steamy Cheese Potato Soup

2 tablespoons butter
1/3 cup chopped celery
1 bunch green onions, chopped
6 cups frozen southern-style hashbrowns, thawed
Two 14-ounce cans chicken broth
1 1/2 cups milk
1 1/2 teaspoons salt
1/2 teaspoon pepper
1/2 teaspoon paprika
2 cups shredded sharp Cheddar cheese
6 slices bacon, cooked and crumbled

Melt the butter in a saucepan over a medium heat. Sauté the celery and onion until tender. Add the hashbrowns and broth. Cover and simmer about 15 minutes or until the hashbrowns are tender. Purée the potato mixture, a small amount at a time, in blender or food processor. Return to the saucepan. Stir in the milk and seasonings. Add the cheese; heat until melted. Garnish with the crumbled bacon.

Serves 6

Tortellini Florentine Soup

3 garlic cloves, minced
1 tablespoon butter
30 ounces chicken broth
8 ounces cheese tortellini, frozen
1/2 teaspoon salt
1/2 teaspoon pepper
1 cup shredded Parmesan cheese
14.5-ounce can stewed tomatoes
1/2 bunch of spinach, washed and stemmed
1/2 tablespoon basil

Sauté the garlic in the butter until tender. Stir in the broth and tortellini; bring to a boil. Reduce the heat. Mix in the Parmesan cheese. Season with the salt and pepper. Simmer until tortellini is just tender. Stir in the tomatoes, spinach and basil. Serve immediately.

Serves 4

Stir frequently, if this sits on the stove for a long period of time, the cheese tends to clump together.

Cream of Tomato Basil Soup

Nothing beats this soup served with a grilled cheese sandwich on a cold winter night.

28-ounce can whole tomatoes
1 cup whipping cream
1 1/2 tablespoons dried basil
1 1/2 tablespoons dried parsley
1 teaspoon pepper
1/4 teaspoon salt
1 cup freshly grated Parmesan cheese

Combine the tomatoes, whipping cream, basil, parsley, pepper and salt in a blender container. Pulse until the mixture is smooth. Pour the mixture into a medium saucepan. Cook over a medium heat until hot. Stir in the cheese; heat until the cheese is melted.

Serves 4

New England Clam Chowder

1 small onion, chopped
1 stick butter
Three 10.5-ounce cans clam chowder
Four 10.5-ounce cans potato soup
Two 6.5-ounce cans minced clams, drained
1/2 gallon half-and-half

Sauté the onion in the butter. Add the soups, clams and half-and-half. Bring to a boil. Reduce heat and simmer for 4 hours.

Serves 10

Vegetable Chili

10-ounce can tomatoes with green chiles
15-ounce can black beans
15-ounce can kidney beans
15-ounce can Great Northern beans
28-ounce can chopped tomatoes
4.5-ounce can chopped green chiles
1 teaspoon minced garlic
1 medium zucchini, sliced
1 medium yellow squash, sliced
1 green bell pepper, chopped
1 medium onion, chopped
7-ounce can sliced mushrooms
1 teaspoon dried oregano
2 tablespoons chili powder
1/2 teaspoon cumin
1/2 teaspoon sugar

Combine all of the ingredients in a stockpot. Bring to a
boil; reduce the heat and simmer for 3 hours. Add 1 cup
of water if it is too thick.

Serves 8

Taco Soup

I pound ground beef
I medium onion, chopped
Two 2.5-ounce packages taco seasoning
Two I-ounce packages dry ranch dressing
I cup beer
15-ounce can black beans, drained
15-ounce can kidney beans, drained
10-ounce can diced tomatoes with green chiles
12-ounce can white Shoe Peg corn
46-ounce can tomato juice

Brown the beef; add the onion. Dissolve the taco seasoning and ranch mix in the beer. Pour over the meat mixture. Add the beans, tomatoes, corn, and tomato juice. Bring to a boil; reduce the heat and simmer for at least 30 minutes.

Serves 4

For a vegetarian alternative omit the meat and tomato juice then double the amount of beans.

Corn Chowder

6 slices bacon, chopped
2 onions, chopped
1/4 cup water
2 large potatoes, diced
1/2 teaspoon salt
1/2 teaspoon pepper
14.75-ounce can cream-style corn
2 cups milk

Cook the bacon and onions in a large skillet until brown. Add the water, potatoes, salt and pepper. Cook until the potatoes are done. Add the corn and milk; heat thoroughly without boiling.

Serves 4

Onion Soup

4 onions, thinly sliced
1 stick butter
1 tablespoon all-purpose flour
2 ounces white wine
14.5-ounce can chicken broth
14.5-ounce can beef broth
1/2 teaspoon salt
1/2 teaspoon pepper
4 slices packaged garlic cheese bread, frozen

Sauté the onions in the butter until slightly brown. Add the flour; stir well. Add the wine, chicken broth, beef broth, salt and pepper; allow to boil for 15 minutes. Cook the bread according to the package directions. Cut the bread in half and place a piece on top of the soup in the bowls.

Serves 6

Anne Grace's Corn Salad

Two 12-ounce cans Shoe Peg corn, drained
2 tomatoes, seeded, drained and chopped
1 bell pepper, seeded and chopped
1 cucumber, peeled, seeded and chopped
1/2 cup sour cream
4 tablespoons mayonnaise
2 tablespoons vinegar
1/2 teaspoon celery seed
1/2 teaspoon dry mustard
1/2 teaspoon pepper
2 teaspoons salt

Combine the corn, tomatoes, pepper and cucumber.
Combine the sour cream, mayonnaise, vinegar and seasonings. Pour the sauce over the vegetables. Cover and refrigerate overnight.

RICH IN FLAVOR

Black-Eyed Pea Salad

Two 15.8-ounce cans black-eyed peas, drained
1 tablespoon butter
1/2 teaspoon salt
1/4 teaspoon pepper
2/3 cup wine vinegar
1 cup chopped onion
1 tablespoon chopped green pepper
1 1/2 cup oil
1 garlic clove, minced
8-ounce can chopped mushrooms, drained

Bring the peas and butter to a boil in a saucepan; cool. Combine the remaining ingredients in a large bowl. Add the black-eyed peas; toss.

Spinach and Raspberry Dressing

1/4 cup raspberry-cranberrry juice drink
1/4 cup seedless raspberry jam
3 tablespoons raspberry vinegar
2 tablespoons olive oil
1/2 teaspoon salt
1/8 teaspoon freshly ground pepper
4 1/2 cups spinach, washed and stems cut
1/4 cup grated Parmesan cheese

Combine the juice, jam, vinegar, oil, salt and pepper in a bottle; cover tightly and shake vigorously. Place the spinach in a bowl. Drizzle with the raspberry dressing; toss to coat. Sprinkle with the Parmesan cheese and serve immediately.

Any combination of greens will work. The dressing makes this salad!

Salad with Almonds and Orange Dressing

2 cups sliced fresh strawberries
4 cups mixed greens
2 tablespoons sliced almonds, lightly toasted
3/4 cup unsweetened orange juice
2 1/2 teaspoons cornstarch
1 teaspoon vegetable oil
2 teaspoons honey
1/2 teaspoon almond extract

Toss the strawberries, greens and almonds in a salad bowl. Combine the orange juice, cornstarch, oil, honey, and almond extract; simmer and stir frequently. Remove from the heat when slightly thickened. Cool to room temperature. Pour over the greens. Cover and refrigerate any extra dressing.

Cinnamon Apple Salad

Two 3-ounce packages lemon gelatin
1/2 cup red hot cinnamon candies
2 cups boiling water
1-pound jar applesauce
1 tablespoon lemon juice
1/8 teaspoon salt
3 ounces cream cheese, cubed
1/2 cup chopped nuts

Dissolve the gelatin and candies in the boiling water. Add the applesauce, lemon juice and salt. Chill until partially set. Add the cubed cream cheese and nuts. Pour into a 10x6-inch pan. Chill.

Serves 6

Grape Salad

8 ounces sour cream
8 ounces cream cheese, softened
1/2 cup sugar
4 pounds small seedless grapes
1/2 cup brown sugar
1/2 cup chopped pecans

Combine the sour cream, cream cheese and sugar in a bowl; blend well. Add the grapes; stir until coated. Sprinkle with brown sugar and pecans. Refrigerate.

Margarita Pretzel Salad

4 cups crushed mini pretzels
1/2 cup butter, melted
1/2 cup sugar
Two 8-ounce packages cream cheese, softened
1/2 cup frozen margarita mix concentrate, thawed
3-ounce package strawberry gelatin
1/2 cup boiling water
10-ounce package frozen sliced strawberries in syrup
3 cups container whipped topping, thawed
1/2 cup sliced fresh strawberries
1/2 lime, sliced

Combine the pretzels, butter and sugar. Press the mixture into the bottom of a coated 9 x 13-inch baking dish. Bake at 350 degrees for 10 minutes. Cool completely. Combine the cream cheese and margarita mix; beat until well blended. Spread the mixture evenly over the crust; refrigerate. Combine the gelatin in the boiling water, mix until completely dissolved. Add the frozen strawberries; stir until they separate and the gelatin is thickened. Whisk in 3 cups of whipped topping. Pour the gelatin over the cream cheese layer and spread to edges. Refrigerate 3 hours. Garnish with strawberry and lime slices.

Serves 15

Simple Taco Salad

2 pounds ground beef
1.25-ounce package taco seasoning mix
1 head lettuce, torn into bite size pieces
1 large onion, chopped
1 large tomato, chopped
1 1/2 cups shredded Cheddar cheese
1-pound bag tortilla chips, crumbled
16-ounce bottle Thousand Island Salad Dressing

Brown the ground beef; drain. Add the taco seasoning; set aside. Layer the lettuce, onion, tomatoes, ground beef, cheese, chips and the dressing in a large bowl. Pour the dressing on the salad when ready to serve. Toss gently to coat.

Serves 4 to 6

Mandy's Mexican Salad

1 head lettuce, torn into bite-size pieces
1/2 cup shredded Cheddar cheese
1/2 cup chopped green onions
1/2 cup chopped black olives
4 medium tomatoes, sliced
Avocado Dressing
1 cup crushed tortilla chips

Toss the lettuce, cheese, onions, olives and tomatoes. Drizzle the avocado dressing over the top; mix well. Garnish with the tortilla chips.

Avocado Dressing

1 avocado, peeled, pitted and mashed
1 tablespoon lemon juice
1/2 cup sour cream
1/3 cup vegetable oil
1/2 teaspoon sugar
1/2 teaspoon garlic salt
1/2 teaspoon chili powder

Combine all ingredients in a jar; shake well.

Fiesta Pasta Salad

2 cups small rotini noodles
1 cup salsa
1/2 cup mayonnaise
1/2 teaspoon salt
14-ounce can kidney beans
1 cup shredded Mexican cheese
1 cup chopped tomatoes
1 medium red pepper, chopped
10-ounce can whole kernel corn, drained
2.25-ounce can sliced black olives
1/4 cup chopped red onion

Cook the pasta according to the package directions; drain and cool. Place the cooled pasta in a large bowl. Combine the salsa, mayonnaise and salt. Pour over the pasta; mix gently. Add the beans, cheese, tomatoes, pepper, corn, olives and onion. Chill.

This recipe is even better if you make it a day or two ahead of time.

Rice and Artichoke Salad

One 6.9-ounce package chicken-flavored Rice-A-Roni
Two 6-ounce jars artichokes, drained, reserving liquid
2 green onions, sliced
1/2 green pepper, chopped
8 stuffed olives, sliced
1/4 teaspoon curry
1/2 cup mayonnaise
3 chicken breasts, cooked and chopped

Cook the Rice-A-Roni according to the package directions, omitting the butter; set aside to cool. Chop the artichokes. Add the onions, pepper, olives, curry, mayonnaise and chicken. Add to the rice. Let stand for several hours or overnight.

Serves 7

Hot Chicken Salad

2 chicken breast, cooked and chopped
1 cup chopped celery
1/4 cup chopped green pepper
1 cup mayonnaise
1/2 cup milk
3 tablespoons lemon juice
1 cup slivered almonds
1 cup French-fried onions
Paprika

Combine the chicken, celery, pepper, mayonnaise, milk, lemon juice and almonds. Pour into a coated casserole dish. Bake at 350 degrees for 30 minutes. Sprinkle the French- fried onions and paprika over the top. Return to the oven and cook an additional 5 minutes.

Chicken Salad with Wild Rice

10 chicken breasts, cooked and chopped
1 cup finely-chopped celery
8-ounce can sliced water chestnuts, finely chopped
2 cups slivered almonds, toasted
1 tablespoon lemon juice
1 1/2 cups mayonnaise
6-ounce box wild rice, cooked
1 teaspoon garlic salt
1/2 teaspoon pepper
1/2 teaspoon curry

Combine all of the ingredients.

Serves 12

Caesar Salad Dressing

1 tablespoon Worcestershire sauce
2 teaspoons Dijon mustard
4 tablespoons Parmesan cheese
1/4 cup water
1 tablespoon lemon juice
1/2 teaspoon salt
1/4 teaspoon pepper
1/2 cup olive oil
1 garlic clove, minced

Combine the Worcestershire sauce, mustard, cheese, water, lemon juice, salt, pepper and olive oil. Add the garlic; blend. Pour into a small glass jar. Shake vigorously.

Entrées

DIVINE DINING

RICH IN FLAVOR

Chicken Pesto Packages

4 boneless chicken breasts
1.25-ounce packet pesto
1 large tomato, chopped
1/2 cup olive oil
1/2 cup grated Parmesan cheese
17.3-ounce box puffed pastry, thawed

Cook the chicken; cut into bite size pieces. Prepare the pesto according to the package directions. Combine the chicken, tomato, pesto and cheese. Roll the pastry using a rolling pin until fairly thin. Cut each sheet in half. Fill each rectangle with the mixture. Fold the sides up like a package. Place the package seam side down on a coated 9 x 13-inch baking pan; bake at 400 degrees for 20 to 30 minutes until golden.

Serves 4

Chicken and Spinach Bake

9-ounce package prewashed spinach
4 skinless, boneless chicken breasts, uncooked
1/2 teaspoon salt
1/2 teaspoon pepper
2 Roma tomatoes, sliced
1 cup sliced mushrooms
1.4-ounce packet Italian salad dressing mix
Balsamic vinegar
2 cups shredded mozzarella or Parmesan cheese
16-ounce package angel hair pasta or rice, cooked

Place the spinach in the bottom of a coated 9 x 13-inch baking dish. Place the chicken breasts on top of the spinach; season with the salt and pepper. Place the tomatoes and mushrooms on top of the chicken. Mix the Italian salad dressing according to the package directions, substituting the balsamic vinegar for the regular vinegar. Pour the dressing over the spinach, chicken, tomatoes and mushrooms. Top with the cheese. Bake at 350 degrees for 40 minutes. Serve over the angel hair pasta or rice.

Serves 4

My friend Stephanie gave me this recipe and every time I serve it, I am asked for the recipe. I have passed it on more times than I can count. It is simple and can fit into a low-carb diet by serving it with other vegetables rather than with pasta or rice.

Trish's Chicken Enchiladas

The wife of the youth pastor served us this dish when my husband interviewed for a pastoral job in Decatur. Mexican food is my favorite so this meal was superb. The rich avocado sauce makes it stand out above your typical enchilada recipe.

2 cups cooked, chopped chicken
4.5-ounce can chopped green chiles
7-ounces salsa verde (green chili sauce)
6 to 8 flour tortillas
1 ripe avocado
1 pint heavy cream
1/2 teaspoon salt
1 1/2 teaspoon lemon juice
2 cups shredded Monterey Jack cheese

Combine the chicken, chiles and green chili sauce. Spoon the chicken mixture into one tortilla at a time; roll up each tortilla and place in a coated glass baking dish, seam side down. Place the meat of the avocado, cream, salt, and lemon juice into the glass container of a blender; pulse until smooth. Pour over the enchiladas; top with the shredded cheese. Bake at 350 degrees for 20 minutes or until hot and bubbly.

Serves 4 to 6

Nancy's Creamy Baked Chicken

Suitable for freezing.

6 boneless chicken breasts
1/2 teaspoon pepper
12 bacon slices
2.25-ounce package dried beef
Two 10.5-ounce cans cream of chicken soup
1 1/2 cups sour cream
3 ounces cream cheese
4 cups hot rice

Season the chicken with pepper. Wrap the bacon around each chicken breast. Place the layer of dried beef in the bottom of a coated 9 x 13-inch baking dish. Arrange the chicken on the beef slices. Combine the soup, sour cream, and cream cheese; cover the chicken. Cover tightly with aluminum foil. Bake at 350 degrees for 2 hours. When tender, remove the foil and brown slightly. Serve on a bed of hot rice.

Serves 6

Stuffed Chicken Monterey

8 boneless chicken breasts
Two 4.5-ounce cans green chiles
1/2 pound Monterey Jack cheese, cut into 8 strips
1/2 cup bread crumbs
1/4 cup Parmesan cheese, grated
3 teaspoons chili powder
1/4 teaspoon cumin
1/2 teaspoon salt
1/4 teaspoon pepper
6 tablespoons butter, melted

Pound the chicken breast between two sheets of waxed paper until thin. Spread 1 tablespoon of the chiles on each breast. Place a cheese strip on top of the chiles. Roll each breast up and tuck the ends under; secure with a wooden toothpick. Combine the bread crumbs, Parmesan cheese, chili powder, cumin, salt and pepper in a shallow dish. Dip each breast into the melted butter and roll in the bread crumb mixture. Place the breast in a baking dish, seam side down. Drizzle with the remaining butter. Cover and chill for at least 4 hours or overnight. Bake at 400 degrees for 30 minutes or until done. Serve with Tomato Sauce. Garnish with sour cream and fresh limes.

Tomato Sauce

15-ounce can tomato sauce
1/3 cup chopped green onions
1/2 teaspoon cumin
1/2 teaspoon salt
1/2 teaspoon pepper

Combine all of the ingredients in a small saucepan. Bring to a boil. Cook, stirring constantly, until slightly thickened.

Chicken Noodle Bake

5 green onions, chopped
4 tablespoon butter, divided
5 cooked chicken breasts, chopped
20 ounces fettuccini
14.5-ounce can chicken broth
1 cup mayonnaise
1 cup sour cream
10 3/4-ounce can cream of mushroom soup
1 1/2 teaspoons Dijon mustard
3 tablespoons dry sherry
6 ounces Cheddar cheese, grated
Parmesan cheese

This recipe is one of our Once-a-Month-Cooking favorites. It freezes well and the sherry gives it a unique flavor.

Sauté the onions with 2 tablespoons of the butter. Combine the onions and chicken. Cook the fettuccini according to the package directions, using the chicken broth as a substitution for some of the water. Drain the fettuccini and toss with the remaining 2 tablespoons of butter.

Combine the mayonnaise, sour cream, soup, mustard, sherry and Cheddar cheese; mix well. Place the fettuccini in a coated 9 x 13-inch baking dish. Cover with the chicken mixture. Top with the sauce. Sprinkle generously with the Parmesan cheese. Bake at 350 degrees for 35 minutes.

Ginger Chicken

1/4 pound butter
2 green onions, chopped in 1-inch pieces
1 teaspoon powdered ginger
8-ounce can sliced water chestnuts, drained
2 cups chopped, cooked chicken
4-ounce can mushroom caps
1/2 teaspoon salt
1/2 teaspoon pepper
4 tablespoons sour cream

Combine the butter, onions, ginger, chestnuts, chicken, mushrooms, salt and pepper in a large skillet; heat thoroughly. Stir in the sour cream. Serve immediately over rice. Top with additional sour cream.

Serves 4

Easy Alfredo

5-ounce can evaporated milk
2 1/2 cups Parmesan cheese, divided
14.5-ounce can diced tomatoes
2 garlic cloves, minced
3 ounces cream cheese
1/4 cup butter
10-ounces frozen broccoli, cooked
4 chicken breasts, cooked and diced
16-ounce package linguini, cooked
1/2 cup crumbled bacon
Salt
Pepper

Combine the milk, 2 cups of the Parmesan cheese, tomatoes, garlic, cream cheese and butter in a saucepan. Cook over a medium heat for 15 minutes. Add the broccoli and chicken. Pour over the linguini when completely heated. Top with the remaining Parmesan cheese and crumbled bacon. Salt and pepper to taste.

For a variation add sliced mushrooms, substitute shrimp for the chicken and sprinkle with crushed red pepper.

King Ranch Chicken

1 cup chopped onion
1 cup chopped green pepper
1/2 pound sliced mushrooms
1/4 cup butter
10.5-ounce can cream of mushroom soup
10.5-ounce can cream of chicken soup
10 3/4-ounce can diced tomatoes and green chiles
1 garlic clove, minced
2 tablespoons chili powder
12 corn tortillas torn into pieces
2 1/2 cups cooked, diced chicken
1 pound Cheddar cheese, sliced or shredded

Sauté the onion, pepper and mushrooms in the butter in a skillet. Add the soups, tomatoes and green chiles, garlic and chili powder. Line the bottom of a coated 9 x 13-inch pan using the pieces of the tortillas. Spread 1/2 of the chicken over the tortillas and top with 1/2 the sauce, and 1/2 of the cheese. Layer the tortillas, chicken, sauce, and cheese again. Bake at 350 degrees for 30 minutes.

Chicken Divan

20 ounces frozen broccoli, cooked and drained
3 cups cooked chicken
Two 10.5-ounce cans cream of chicken soup
1/2 cup mayonnaise
1 teaspoon lemon juice
1/2 teaspoon curry
2 cups shredded Cheddar cheese
1 sleeve buttered crackers, crushed
1 tablespoon butter

Place the broccoli in the bottom of a coated 9 x 13-inch casserole dish. Layer the chicken over the broccoli. Combine the soup, mayonnaise, lemon juice and curry; pour over the chicken. Sprinkle the cheese on top. Bake at 325 degrees for 30 minutes. Cover the top with cracker crumbs and butter and bake for an additional 5 minutes.

Chicken Marbella

8 chicken breasts, thighs, legs and wings,
skin on, bone in
1 head garlic, minced
4 tablespoons dried oregano
1 teaspoon salt
1/2 teaspoon pepper
1/2 cup red wine vinegar
1/2 cup olive oil
1 cup pitted prunes
1/2 cup pimento-stuffed green olives
1/2 cup capers, with a small amount of juice
4 bay leaves
1/2 cup brown sugar
1 cup white wine
Parsley for garnish

Combine the chicken, garlic, oregano, salt, pepper, vinegar, olive oil, prunes, olives, capers and bay leaves in a large container. Cover and marinate in the refrigerator overnight.

Arrange the chicken in a single layer in 1 or 2 large shallow baking dishes. Spoon the marinade evenly over the chicken. Sprinkle with the brown sugar. Pour the white wine over the top. Bake at 350 degrees for 50 to 60 minutes, basting occasionally with pan juices, until chicken is done. Garnish with parsley.

Poppy Seed Chicken

2 to 3 cups cooked chicken
10.5-ounce can cream of chicken soup
8 ounces sour cream
2 sleeves butter crackers, crushed
3 tablespoons poppy seeds
1/2 stick butter, melted

Place the chicken in the bottom of a coated 9 x 13-inch casserole dish. Combine soup and sour cream; pour over the chicken. Combine the crackers and poppy seeds. Sprinkle over the top. Drizzle the butter over the top. Bake at 350 degrees for 30 minutes.

 y friend, Diane, takes this dish to people in need. Paired with a salad, bread and dessert, it is easy to prepare and it is easy to transport.

Fresh Pesto on Penne

3 garlic cloves
1/4 cup shelled pistachios
1 cup basil leaves, packed
1/4 cup olive oil
1/4 cup Parmesan cheese
1/2 teaspoon Tabasco sauce
3/4 teaspoon soy sauce
1 pound penne pasta

Chop the garlic in a food processor. Add the pistachios, basil, oil, cheese and sauces. Cook the pasta according to the package directions. Add the pesto while the pasta is warm. Serve at room temperature.

Serves 4

Spinach Lasagna

Three friends and I formed a Once-a-Month-Cooking Group. We gather at one of our homes and cook 20 meals-doubling the recipes and placing them in four 8x8 freezer-to-oven pans. It is a great way to save money and time. We also have a great time doing it. This lasagna is a dish that always makes the menu. It freezes well and is a hearty alternative to a meat lasagna.

1 large onion, chopped
1 cup sliced mushrooms
4 garlic cloves, minced
2 tablespoons butter
6-ounce jar of artichokes, chopped
12-ounce jar roasted red peppers
10-ounce package frozen spinach, thawed
15 ounces ricotta cheese
1 1/2 cups shredded mozzarella cheese
1 cup grated Parmesan cheese, divided
2 eggs, beaten
2 teaspoons dried basil
1 teaspoon dried oregano
1/2 teaspoon pepper
32 ounces spaghetti sauce
9 lasagna noodles

Cook the onion, mushrooms and garlic in the butter until tender in a large skillet. Stir in the artichokes and red peppers. Pat the spinach dry. Combine the spinach, ricotta cheese, mozzarella cheese, 1/2 cup of the Parmesan cheese, eggs, basil, oregano and pepper. Stir the pepper-artichoke mixture into the spinach mixture. Pour 16 ounces of sauce in the bottom of 9 x 13-inch baking dish. Cover with the uncooked noodles, layer the spinach mixture, sauce and remaining Parmesan cheese. Bake, covered, at 375 for 20 minutes. Uncover and bake an additional 10 minutes. Let stand for 10 minutes.

Serves 6

Manicotti

8-ounce package of jumbo "manicotti" shells
16 ounces of ricotta cheese
1 cup grated Parmesan cheese, divided
2 cups mozzarella cheese, divided
2 eggs, beaten
2 teaspoons salt, divided
2 teaspoons pepper, divided
1 medium onion, chopped
2 tablespoons olive oil
15-ounce can tomato sauce
12-ounce can tomato paste
1 bay leaf

Boil the shells for 7 minutes over a medium heat. Combine the ricotta cheese, 1/2 cup of the Parmesan cheese, 1 cup of mozzarella cheese, eggs, 1 teaspoon of the salt and 1 teaspoon of the pepper. Place the cheese mixture in a resealable bag; seal and cut the corner. Squeeze the cheese mixture into each shell.

Sauté the onion and garlic in the olive oil. Add the tomato sauce and tomato paste. Fill each can with water; pour into the mixture. Add the bay leaf, the remaining salt and pepper; simmer for 2 hours. Place 2 cups of sauce in the bottom of a 9 x 13-inch baking dish. Layer noodles, more sauce, remaining Parmesan and mozzarella cheeses. Bake at 350 degrees for 45 minutes.

Bean Burritos

Two 16-ounce cans refried beans
2.5-ounce package taco seasoning
10 3/4-ounce can diced tomatoes with green chiles
8 flour tortillas
1 onion, chopped
2 cups shredded Cheddar cheese
1 tomato, chopped
1 cup chopped lettuce
1 cup sour cream
1 cup salsa

Combine the beans, taco seasoning and tomatoes with green chiles in a medium saucepan. Cook over a medium heat until warm. Warm the tortillas according to the package directions. Spoon 1/2 cup of the bean mixture in the center of tortillas, sprinkle with the onion and cheese. Wrap the burritos and place seam side down in a greased 9 x 13-inch baking dish. Cover with the remaining cheese. Bake at 350 degrees for 10 minutes. Remove from the oven and top with the tomato, lettuce, sour cream and salsa.

Makes 8 burritos

Alabama Jammin' Jambalaya

1 pound sliced smoked sausage
1 pound cooked chicken breast, diced
1 bunch green onions, chopped
3 stalks celery, chopped
1/2 cup chopped green pepper
1 cup chopped parsley
2 cups converted rice, uncooked
10.5-ounce can French onion soup
8-ounce can mushroom stems and pieces, drained
1/2 stick of butter
2 cups diced tomatoes and green chilies
1/2 teaspoon pepper
1 teaspoon Worcestershire sauce
1/2 teaspoon red pepper
1 pound shrimp, peeled and deveined

Brown the sausage; add the chicken and cook for 5 minutes. Add the onions, celery, green pepper, parsley, rice, soup, mushrooms, butter, tomatoes and green chiles and seasonings; bring to a boil. Add the shrimp. Place in a roasting pan and cover. Bake at 350 degrees for 15 minutes; stir and cook an additional 15 minutes. Remove from the oven and let sit covered for 30 minutes covered.

Serves 8

My friend Donna recommends this recipe. At Supper Clubs or Birthday Clubs this recipe is popular because you can easily prepare it for a large crowd.

This is a great make-ahead meal. Double the recipe and bake the okra mixture for two hours, allow it to cool and then freeze in two resealable freezer(Must say freezer because other bags will allow mixture to spoil over time) bags. Combine frozen mixture with broth and tomatoes adding shrimp at the end of the cooking time when ready to serve.

Okra Gumbo

1 pound fresh okra, sliced
1 1/2 medium onions, chopped
1 celery rib, chopped
1/2 green bell pepper, chopped
1/2 garlic clove, minced
6 ounces tomato sauce
1 bay leaf
1 1/2 teaspoons salt
2 teaspoons pepper
32 ounces chicken broth
14-ounce can diced tomatoes
1 pound raw shrimp, peeled and deveined
3 cups cooked rice

Combine the okra, onions, celery, pepper, garlic, tomato sauce, bay leaf, salt and pepper. Spoon the mixture into an 8 x 8-inch baking dish; cover with aluminum foil. Bake at 300 degrees for 2 hours, stirring after 1 hour. Remove from the baking dish; combine the mixture with chicken broth and diced tomatoes in a stock pot. Bring to a boil; reduce to a simmer, covered for 1 hour. Add shrimp and cook until the shrimp turn pink. Discard the bay leaf. Serve over rice.

Serves 4

Mrs. Ashley's Shrimp and Crab Casserole

1/4 onion, chopped
1 tablespoon butter
1 pound crab meat
1 pound shrimp
3 hard-boiled eggs, chopped
1 garlic clove
10 3/4-ounce can cream of mushroom soup
10 3/4-ounce can cream of chicken soup
8 ounces sour cream
3/4 cup mayonnaise
1 cup grated Parmesan cheese
1 tablespoon pimento
1/2 teaspoon salt
1/4 teaspoon pepper
Bread crumbs
Slivered almonds

I have friends from Kentucky who travel each spring and fall to Gulf Shores where they own condominiums. They stop at our house to visit on the way down or way back. They love the Alabama coast and have been coming here for years. This recipe was given to them from an Alabama native. It is fun to see that Alabama is enjoyed by more than just her own residents.

Sauté the onion in the butter in a skillet. Toss with the crab meat, shrimp, eggs and garlic. Combine the soups, sour cream, mayonnaise, Parmesan cheese, pimento, salt and pepper. Pour all of the ingredients into a coated 9 x 13-inch baking dish. Top with the bread crumbs and slivered almonds. Bake at 350 degrees for 30 minutes or until bubbly.

Alabama
RICH IN FLAVOR

Shrimp Scampi Fettucini

1 1/2 pounds fettuccini noodles
2 garlic cloves, minced
2 sticks butter
1/2 cup olive oil
1 1/2 pounds raw shrimp, peeled and deviened
2 teaspoons garlic salt
2 tablespoons dried parsley
Parmesan cheese
Red pepper

Cook the noodles; drain and set aside. Sauté the garlic in the butter and oil. Add the shrimp and salt; cook until the shrimp are pink. Pour over the noodles; add the parsley and toss. Serve with the Parmesan cheese and red pepper.

Serves 4

Shrimp and Grits

4 tablespoons butter
4 cups water
1 cup stone-ground grits
Salt
Pepper
Cajun Shrimp Sauce

Place butter and water in a medium-size pot; bring to a boil. Add the grits; stir until there are no lumps. Return to a boil; reduce heat and cook until grits are tender or about 10 minutes. Stir frequently; add the salt and pepper to taste. Place grits on serving plates; spoon Cajun Shrimp Sauce over the grits. Serve with cornbread.

Makes 6 servings

Cajun Shrimp Sauce

3 cups heavy whipping cream
3 cups sliced mushrooms
1 1/2 cups chopped green onions
1 tablespoon Dijon mustard
2 teaspoons blackening spice
2 pounds raw shrimp, peeled and deveined

Heat the heavy cream on medium to high heat in a large saucepan. Add the mushrooms, onions, mustard and blackening spice. Cook until the cream starts to thicken; add shrimp. Cook until shrimp is pink and cooked through.

Linguini with Clam Sauce

1 cup chopped celery
1 onion chopped
2 garlic cloves
1 tablespoon olive oil
28-ounce can diced tomatoes
6.5-ounce can minced clams, drained,
reserving liquid
1 tablespoon parsley
1 tablespoon oregano
1 teaspoon basil
1/2 teaspoon salt
1/2 cup white cooking wine
1 tablespoon butter
1 pound linguini noodles, cooked
1/2 teaspoon crushed red pepper

Sauté the celery, onion and garlic in the olive oil. Add the tomatoes, clams, parsley, oregano, basil, salt and 1/2 cup liquid from the clams. Bring to a boil; reduce heat and simmer for 20 minutes. Add the wine and cook an additional 10 minutes. Place the butter in the sauce and let melt. Serve over noodles; sprinkle with red pepper.

Cajun Burgers

1 pound ground beef
1 cup chopped onion
4 tablespoons mustard
4 tablespoons ketchup
10.5-ounce can chicken gumbo soup
1/2 teaspoon salt
1/2 teaspoon pepper

Brown the ground beef in a skillet; drain. Add the onion, mustard, ketchup, soup, salt and pepper. Simmer for 15 to 20 minutes. Serve on toasted hamburger buns.

Serves 6

Deep Dish Pizza

I serve this often at casual get-togethers. It makes a heavy casserole of meat and bread so I only have to prepare a salad and dessert to go with it.

Large Chef Boyardee cheese pizza kit
1 pound ground beef or ground turkey
1/2 green pepper, chopped
1 medium onion, chopped
14.5-ounce can diced tomatoes
1/2 teaspoon salt
1/2 teaspoon pepper
1/4 teaspoon garlic salt
1 tablespoon oregano
1/2 tablespoon basil
3 cups shredded mozzarella cheese, divided

Prepare the crust according to the package directions. Brown the beef; drain. Add the pepper and onion; cook until soft. Add the tomato sauce from the kit as well as the diced tomatoes and seasonings. Simmer for 15 to 20 minutes. Press the dough into the bottom of a coated 9 x 13-inch glass baking dish. Layer 1 cup of mozzarella cheese, sauce, 1 cup of mozzarella cheese, remaining sauce, the remaining mozzarella cheese and the packet of Parmesan cheese from the kit. Bake at 350 degrees for 25 to 30 minutes. Let cool for 5 minutes before serving.

Serves 6

Taco Lasagna

1 1/2 pounds ground beef
1 cup chopped onion
1 1/2 cups chopped green pepper
4.5-ounce can green chiles
2.5-ounce package taco seasoning
2 cups taco sauce
3 cups Colby/Jack cheese
10 flour tortillas

Brown the ground beef. Add the onion, pepper, chiles and taco seasoning. Spread 1/2 cup of the taco sauce in the bottom of a coated 9 x 13-inch casserole dish. Layer with 5 of the tortillas, folded in half to fit across the dish. Layer with 1/2 of the meat mixture, 1 cup of the taco sauce, 1 1/2 cups of the cheese; repeat again. Bake at 375 degrees for 15 to 20 minutes or until the cheese is melted.

Serves 6

Baked Spaghetti

1 cup chopped onion
1 cup chopped green pepper
1 tablespoon butter
28-ounce can diced tomatoes
4-ounce can mushrooms, drained
2.25-ounce can sliced olives, drained
2 teaspoons dried oregano
1 pound ground beef, browned
12 ounces spaghetti, cooked and drained
8 ounces shredded Cheddar cheese
10.5-ounce can cream of mushroom soup
1/4 cup water
1/4 cup grated Parmesan cheese

Sauté the onions and green pepper in the butter in a skillet until tender. Add the tomatoes, mushrooms, olives, oregano, and ground beef. Simmer uncovered for 10 minutes. Place 1/2 of the spaghetti in the bottom of a coated 9 x 13-inch glass baking dish. Top with 1/2 of the meat mixture and 1 cup of the Cheddar cheese; repeat. Combine the soup and water until smooth; pour over the top. Sprinkle with the Parmesan cheese. Bake at 350 degrees for 30 to 35 minutes.

ME GROWN VEGETABLES

BESS'S
FRESH PRODUCE
HOME GROWN VEGETABLES
APPLES

Be
TOMATOES
ONIONS
SQUASH

SWEET
POTATOES
$3⁰⁰

Kins
1.00

Cheeseburger Pie

1 pound ground beef
1 1/2 teaspoons salt, divided
1/2 teaspoon oregano
1/2 teaspoon pepper
1/2 cup bread crumbs
8 ounces tomato sauce
1/2 cup chopped onion
1/2 cup chopped green pepper
9-inch deep dish unbaked pie shell
1 egg
1/2 teaspoon dry mustard
1/2 teaspoon Worcestershire sauce
2 cups shredded cheddar cheese
1/4 cup milk

Brown the beef; drain. Add 1 teaspoon of the salt, oregano, pepper, bread crumbs, tomato sauce, onion and green pepper. Pour into the pie shell. Combine the egg, mustard, Worcestershire sauce, cheese and milk. Spread over the meat mixture. Bake at 425 degrees for 25 minutes.

Meatloaf with Fresh Veggies

1 1/2 pounds lean ground beef
1 cup Italian-seasoned bread crumbs
1 carrot, peeled and grated
1 zucchini, grated
1/2 red pepper, chopped
1/2 onion, chopped
2 garlic cloves, minced
1/4 cup chicken broth
1 egg, beaten
1/4 cup ketchup
1 teaspoon dried basil
1 tablespoon Dijon mustard
1/2 teaspoon salt
1/2 teaspoon pepper

Combine all of the ingredients. Place in a coated loaf pan. Bake at 350 degrees for 45 to 50 minutes.

Serves 6

Baked Ziti

1 1/2 pounds penne pasta
1/2 pound ground beef
1 cup chopped onion
1 cup green pepper
2.25-ounce can sliced black olives, drained
26-ounce jar spaghetti sauce
1 1/2 cups mozzarella cheese, divided
1/2 cup grated Parmesan cheese

Cook the pasta according to package directions. Brown the beef; drain. Add the onion and green pepper; sauté the vegetables. Add the olives and spaghetti sauce; simmer for 15 minutes. Add the noodles and 1/2 cup mozzarella cheese; mix well. Pour into a coated 9 x 13-inch casserole dish. Cover the ziti with the remaining cheeses. Bake, covered, at 350 degrees for 25 minutes.

Coca-Cola Roast

2 pound sirloin roast
1 onion, chopped
15-ounce can beef broth
10 3/4-ounce can cream of mushroom soup
12-ounce can Coca-Cola
1 envelope onion soup mix

Sauté the roast and onion in cooking spray until the roast is seared on both sides. Add the broth, soup, Coca-Cola and onion soup mix. Simmer covered for several hours or until tender.

Sides

COLORFUL COMPANION

Pineapple Side

1 cup sugar
6 tablespoons all-purpose flour
6 tablespoons pineapple juice,
reserved from canned pineapple
Two 20-ounce cans pineapple chunks
1 1/2 cups shredded Cheddar cheese
1 stick butter
1 sleeve butter crackers, crushed

Combine the sugar, flour and reserved pineapple juice. Add the pineapple chunks and cheese; mix well. Pour into a 2-quart baking dish. Combine the butter and crackers; sprinkle on top. Bake at 350 degrees for 20 to 30 minutes.

Serves 6

Corn Casserole

7-ounce can whole kernel corn, drained
Two 8 3/4-ounce cans cream-style corn
1 cup crushed butter crackers
1/4 cup chopped onion
1/2 cup shredded processed cheese
1 teaspoon salt
2 eggs, beaten
2 tablespoons butter, melted
1/4 teaspoon paprika
1 cup milk

Combine all of the ingredients; mix well. Pour into a coated 1 1/2-quart casserole dish. Bake at 350 degrees for 50 to 55 minutes or until knife inserted in the center comes out clean.

Serves 10

Alabama
RICH IN FLAVOR

*T*his rice serves
well with
Trish's Chicken
Enchiladas.

Mexican Rice

1 garlic clove, minced
1 cup chopped onion
2 tablespoons butter
1/2 cup tomato sauce
4 cups chicken broth
2 cups long grain rice
1 teaspoon oregano
1 tablespoon marjoram
1 1/2 teaspoons salt
1 teaspoon cumin
1/3 cup chili powder

Sauté the garlic and onion in the butter. Add the tomato sauce, chicken broth, rice and seasonings. Bring to a boil and cook for two minutes. Cover and simmer for 20 to 25 minutes or until the water evaporates.

Serves 6

Pomegranate Pilaf

1 pomegranate
6-ounce package rice pilaf
1/2 cup sliced green onions
1/4 cup pine nuts, toasted
1/4 cup shredded Parmesan cheese

Open the pomegranate; run under cool water and remove arils. Discard the peel and membrane; set aside arils. Prepare the rice pilaf according to the package directions. Stir in the pomegranate arils, green onions, pine nuts and cheese during the last five minutes of cooking.

Serves 4

Fried Green Tomatoes

1 1/2 cups self-rising flour, divided
1 1/2 cups buttermilk
2 large eggs, beaten
1 teaspoon salt, divided
1 teaspoon black pepper, divided
3 green tomatoes
2 cups vegetable oil

Whisk 1 tablespoon of the flour, buttermilk, eggs, 1/2 teaspoon of the salt and 1/2 teaspoon of the pepper in a small bowl. Combine the remaining flour, salt and pepper in a separate bowl. Slice the green tomatoes. Dip the tomato slices in the wet mixture and then in the dry mixture. Fry in oil at 375 degrees until golden brown on each side. Drain on paper towels.

We have a pomegranate tree outside of our house that yields plenty of pomegranates for the whole neighborhood. It took much research to find out the best way to prepare them and this was my first recipe to incorporate this unique fruit. I now use them on salads as well as juice them. The children love them and the arils are such a pretty shade of red that they add color to any dish.

Alabama Scramble

2 cups yellow squash
1 cup zucchini squash
2 cups white potatoes
2 cups okra
Cornmeal
Salt
Pepper

Cut the vegetables into small chunks. Place in a large bowl; coat with the cornmeal. Fry the vegetables in oil until golden brown. Sprinkle with salt and pepper; drain and serve

Organized Green Beans

1 pound bacon
Two 14.5-ounce cans whole green beans
16-ounce bottle Light Catalina dressing

Cut the bacon strips in half. Wrap 6 beans with a piece of the bacon and secure using a wooden toothpick. Repeat until all the beans are wrapped. Place the bundles in a single layer in a 9 x 13-inch baking dish. Pour the dressing over the top; allow to marinate in the refrigerator for several hours. Bake at 400 degrees until the bacon is done.

As crazy as it sounds, the Light Catalina is the key to this recipe. The taste is much better than regular Catalina dressing.

Spinach Madeline

Serves better the next day!

Two 10-ounce packages frozen chopped spinach
2 tablespoons chopped onion
4 tablespoons butter
2 tablespoons all-purpose flour
1/2 cup evaporated milk
1/2 teaspoon pepper
3/4 teaspoon garlic salt
6 ounces jalapeño cheese spread
1 teaspoon Worcestershire sauce
1 cup French-fried onions

Cook the spinach; drain and reserve the liquid. Sauté the onion in the butter. Add the flour and blend well. Add 1/2 cup of the reserved liquid and evaporated milk slowly; stirring constantly. Season with the pepper and garlic salt. Add the cheese spread; stir until smooth. Add the Worcestershire sauce; mix well. Add the spinach; mix well. Top with the French-fried onions.

Vegetable Pie

I pound fresh mushrooms, sliced
I onion, sliced
I zucchini, sliced
I yellow squash, sliced
1/2 green pepper, sliced
3 tablespoons butter
I teaspoon salt
1/2 teaspoon pepper
9-inch deep-dish pie shell, unbaked
I tomato, sliced
I cup mayonnaise
I cup mozzarella cheese

Sauté the mushrooms, onions, zucchini, squash and green pepper in the butter; drain. Add the salt and pepper. Bake the pie shell for 5 minutes. Place the tomato slices in the bottom of the pie shell. Add the sautéed vegetables. Combine the mayonnaise and mozzarella cheese. Spread the mayonnaise mixture over the vegetables. Bake, uncovered, at 325 degrees for 45 minutes.

Black Beans and Rice

15-ounce can black beans, drained
10 ounces frozen corn
2 cups long grain rice, uncooked
16 ounces salsa
1 1/2 cups tomato juice
1/2 teaspoon cumin
1/2 teaspoon oregano
1 cup Cheddar cheese

This recipe freezes well. For a great vegetarian meal, serve with bread.

Combine the beans, corn, rice, salsa, tomato juice, cumin and oregano in a large bowl. Pour into a coated 1 1/2-quart casserole dish. Bake at 375 for 1 hour. Cover with the cheese and cook for 10 more minutes.

Serves 4

Spicy Baked Beans

28-ounce can homestyle baked beans
15-ounce can chili
1 tablespoon prepared mustard
1 tablespoon Creole seasoning
1 tablespoon brown sugar
1 small onion, chopped
1/2 teaspoon paprika
1 teaspoon chili powder
1/2 teaspoon onion powder
1/2 teaspoon garlic powder
1/4 teaspoon black pepper

Combine all of the ingredients; mix well. Pour into a coated 7 x 11 glass casserole dish. Bake at 350 degrees for 35 to 45 minutes.

Marinated Carrots

2 pounds baby carrots
1 onion, thinly sliced
1 small green pepper, thinly sliced
10.5-ounce can tomato soup
1/2 cup vegetable oil
3/4 cup cider vinegar
1 cup sugar
1 teaspoon prepared mustard
1 teaspoon Worcestershire sauce
1 teaspoon salt
1 teaspoon pepper

Cook the carrots until tender; drain and cool. Arrange the carrots, onion and pepper slices in layers in a deep bowl. Combine the soup, oil, vinegar, sugar, mustard, Worcestershire sauce, salt and pepper in a blender. Pour over the carrots, onions and peppers. Cover and let marinate for 24 hours in the refrigerator. May be served hot or cold.

Serves 20

Sweet Potato Supreme

1 1/2 sticks butter, divided
2 cups cooked and mashed sweet potatoes
1 cup sugar
3/4 teaspoon salt, divided
2 eggs
1/2 cup milk
1 1/2 teaspoons vanilla extract
1/2 cup coconut
1/2 cup all-purpose flour
1 cup packed brown sugar
1 cup chopped pecans

Melt 1 stick of the butter. Combine the butter, potatoes, sugar, 1/2 teaspoon of the salt, eggs, milk, vanilla extract, and coconut. Pour into a coated 2-quart casserole dish. Melt the remaining butter. Combine the flour, brown sugar, nuts, butter and the remaining salt; stir until crumbly. Sprinkle over the potato mixture. Bake at 350 degrees for 30 minutes.

Serves 8

Broccoli Casserole

Two 10-ounce boxes frozen chopped broccoli
10.5-ounce can cream of mushroom soup
1 cup shredded, sharp Cheddar cheese
2 eggs, beaten
1 cup mayonnaise
1 sleeve butter crackers, crumbled
1 tablespoon butter, melted

Cook the broccoli according to the package directions; drain. Combine the broccoli, soup, cheese, eggs and mayonnaise. Place in a coated 2-quart casserole dish. Cook at 350 degrees for 25 minutes. Pour the crumbled crackers and butter over the top; return to the oven for 5 minutes.

Butternut Squash Casserole

1 large butternut squash
2 tablespoons butter
1/2 cup dark brown sugar
1/3 cup raisins
1 1/2 cups miniature marshmallows

Slice the squash into quarters and boil until tender; remove the squash from the water. Scrape the pulp from the outer shells; discard the shells. Combine the squash, butter and brown sugar in a bowl; mix until smooth and has the consistency of mashed potatoes. Add the raisins. Fold the mixture into a coated 2-quart casserole dish. Top with the miniature marshmallows. Bake at 400 degrees until the marshmallows are golden brown.

Serves 8

Fried Eggplant Sticks

1 large eggplant
6 tablespoons grated Parmesan cheese
2 eggs, beaten
2 tablespoons milk
3/4 cup fine bread crumbs
Salt
Pepper

Peel and cut the eggplant into 1/2 inch strips. Soak in cold water for 15 minutes. Combine the cheese, eggs and milk. Dip the eggplant strips in the egg mixture and then into the bread crumbs. Fry in hot oil at 375 degrees. Sprinkle with the salt and pepper; drain and serve.

Serves 4

RICH IN FLAVOR

Rosemary Potatoes

4 large potatoes
3 tablespoons butter
1/3 cup sour cream
1/3 cup Parmesan cheese
1 teaspoon dried rosemary
1/2 teaspoon chives
1/2 teaspoon parsley
1/4 teaspoon sage
1/2 teaspoon salt
1/4 teaspoon pepper

Bake the potatoes until done; slice lengthwise. Scoop out the pulp; reserving the skins. Mash the pulp, butter, sour cream, and Parmesan cheese. Add the rosemary, chives, parsley, sage, salt and pepper; blend well. Place the mixture into the potato skins. Wrap in aluminum foil and chill for 1 hour. Reheat at 450 degrees for 25 minutes.

Serves 8

Squash Casserole

1 1/2 pounds squash, diced
1 medium onion, diced
2 tablespoons butter
1/2 teaspoon pepper
1 teaspoon salt
4.5-ounce can chopped green chilies
1 tablespoon all-purpose flour
1 1/2 cups Monterey Jack cheese
1 egg
1 cup cottage cheese
2 tablespoons parsley
1/2 cup Parmesan cheese

Sauté the squash and onion in the butter. Add the pepper, salt, chiles and flour. Place the squash in a coated 2-quart casserole dish. Sprinkle the Monterey Jack cheese over the top. Combine the egg, cottage cheese and parsley. Pour over the Monterey Jack cheese. Sprinkle the Parmesan cheese on top. Bake at 400 degrees for 25 to 30 minutes.

Carrot Soufflé

1 1/2 pounds carrots, sliced
1/2 cup butter
3 eggs
1/4 cup all-purpose flour
1 1/2 teaspoons baking powder
1 cup sugar
1/4 teaspoon cinnamon

Cook the carrots in the butter in a skillet for 20 to 25 minutes; drain. Place the carrots, eggs, flour, baking powder, sugar and cinnamon in a food processor; blend until smooth. Pour into a coated 1 1/2- quart casserole dish. Bake at 350 degrees for 1 hour and 10 minutes or until set.

Cookies/Candies

TASTY TREASURES

Peppermint Fudge

8 ounces cream cheese, softened
4 cups confectioners' sugar
1 1/2 teaspoons vanilla extract
12-ounce package white chocolate chips
1 cup crushed peppermint sticks

Combine the cream cheese, confectioners' sugar and vanilla extract; beat using an electric mixer until smooth. Melt the white chocolate chips in the microwave. Fold into the cream cheese mixture; beat again until smooth. Add the peppermint; stir until well blended. Spread into an 8 x 8-inch coated pan. Chill and cut.

Martha's Toffee Candy

I make this every Christmas. It makes a great gift in a Christmas tin. It is by far one of the easiest candy recipes I've made.

12-ounce package milk chocolate chips
2 cups sliced roasted almonds
2 sticks butter
1 cup sugar
3 tablespoons water

Place 1/2 of the chips and almonds in a coated 9 x 13-inch baking dish. Combine the butter, sugar and water in a saucepan; cook to the hard crack stage, 300 degrees. Pour over the chips and almonds. Add the remaining chips and almonds; smoothing out the chocolate chips. Allow to harden and break into pieces.

Chocolate Pecan Drops

3 cups chopped pecans
3 tablespoons butter
6 squares chocolate bark

Toast the pecans and butter at 300 degrees for 25 minutes; stir twice. Melt the chocolate in the microwave or the top of a double broiler. Combine the chocolate with the pecans, drop by the spoonfuls onto waxed paper. Allow to cool at least 1 hour before packaging or serving.

Simple Peanut Brittle

1/2 cup light molasses
2 cups sugar
1/2 cup brown sugar
1/2 cup water
1/4 cup butter
1/8 teaspoon baking soda
1 1/2 cups salted peanuts

Combine the molasses, sugars, water and butter in a heavy saucepan. Cook, stirring frequently, until 300 degrees is reached on a candy thermometer. Remove from the heat and quickly stir in the baking soda and peanuts. Pour onto a coated baking sheet. Stretch out thin. Cool and break into pieces.

Makes 1 pound

Cookies for Your Sweetheart

My friend Cindy made up this recipe in high school for her boyfriend. Though the relationship ended decades ago, the delicious cookie lives on.

2 cups margarine
2 cups brown sugar
2 cups sugar
2 teaspoons vanilla extract
4 eggs
3 cups sifted all-purpose flour
2 teaspoons salt
2 teaspoons baking soda
5 cups oats
1 1/2 cups crisp rice cereal
2 cups coconut
Two 12-ounce packages semisweet chocolate chips

Combine the margarine, sugars, vanilla extract and eggs. Combine the flour, salt and baking soda in a separate bowl. Combine the dry and wet mixture. Add oats, cereal, coconut and chocolate chips; combine well. Drop by spoonfuls onto a coated baking sheet. Bake at 350 degrees for 10 minutes.

Makes a large batch of cookies

Scottish Shortbread

1/2 pound butter, softened
3/4 cup sugar
1 egg yolk, at room temperature
2 cups all-purpose flour, sifted
1/2 cup rice flour

Whip the butter, sugar and egg yolk in a bowl; add the sifted flour gradually; mixing with your hand. Flatten the dough using a rolling pin. Cut into squares with a pastry cutter. Prick the squares using a fork. Place on a lightly-coated baking sheet. Bake at 350 degrees for 20 minutes.

Gingersnaps

3/4 cup shortening
1 cup brown sugar
1 egg
1/3 cup molasses
2 1/4 cups all-purpose flour
2 teaspoons baking soda
1 teaspoon cinnamon
1 teaspoon ginger
1/2 teaspoon cloves
1/4 teaspoon salt
Sugar

Combine the shortening, brown sugar, egg and molasses; beat well. Add the flour, baking soda, cinnamon, ginger, clove, and salt; mix well. Cover and chill for at least 1 hour. Shape the chilled dough into balls. Dip each ball in the sugar. Place on a lightly-coated baking sheet. Bake at 375 degrees for 10 to 12 minutes. Remove immediately.

Cake Mix Cookies

18.25-ounce box yellow cake mix
1/2 cup vegetable oil
2 eggs, beaten
2 1/2 tablespoons water
1/2 cup semisweet chocolate chips
1/2 cup butterscotch chips

Combine the cake mix, oil, eggs and water. Stir in the chips. Drop the batter by spoonfuls about 2 inches a part on a greased cookie sheet. Bake at 350 degrees for 10 to 12 minutes. Remove from the oven and let cool. Makes 3 dozen cookies.

Kelly's Chocolate Chip Cookies

This recipe came from my friend Kelly who says one key to baking the perfect cookie is to take them out of the oven when they are not quite done cooking. Allow them to cool completely on the baking sheet so they finish cooking outside the oven.

2 cups butter, softened
2 cups brown sugar
2 cups sugar
4 eggs
2 teaspoons vanilla extract
4 cups all-purpose flour
5 cups rolled oats, blended into a powder
1 teaspoon salt
2 teaspoons baking soda
2 teaspoons baking powder
24 ounces semisweet chocolate chips
3 cups chopped walnuts

Cream the butter and sugars together. Add the eggs and vanilla extract. Add the flour, oats, salt, baking soda and baking powder; mix well. Add the chocolate chips and walnuts; mix well. Roll the dough into balls; place the balls 2 inches apart on a coated baking sheet or baking stone. Bake at 375 degrees for 10 minutes.

Makes 112 cookies

Oatmeal-Cranberry-Walnut Cookies

4 tablespoons margarine, softened
1 cup brown sugar
1/2 cup applesauce
1 egg, beaten
2 tablespoons molasses
2 tablespoons water
1 teaspoon vanilla extract
2 cups rolled oats
1 cup whole wheat pastry flour
1/2 teaspoon cinnamon
1/2 teaspoon nutmeg
1/2 teaspoon salt
1/2 teaspoon baking powder
1/2 cup diced walnuts
1 cup dried cranberries

Combine the margarine and brown sugar. Add the apple-sauce, egg, molasses, water and vanilla extract. Combine oats, flour, cinnamon, nutmeg, salt and baking powder in a separate bowl. Fold in the walnuts and cranberries. Combine the wet and dry mixtures. Cover and chill for 30 minutes. Place dough by spoonfuls onto a coated baking sheet. Bake at 375 degrees for 20 minutes or until light brown. Cool for 10 minutes before serving.

Makes 12 large cookies

This is an old recipe from Doris Marie Bowling, the grandmother of my friend Cindy. Mrs. Bowling passed away at 98 but while in her 90's she would prepare these cookies and tell her granddaughter that she was making them for the "old" people at church.

Granny's Rolled Oatmeal Cookies

1 cup margarine
2 cups sugar
2 eggs
2 cups rolled oats
1 teaspoon cinnamon
1 teaspoon salt
3 cups all-purpose flour
1 teaspoon baking soda
2 tablespoons buttermilk
1 cup raisins
Sugar

Combine the margarine, sugar and eggs. Combine the oats, cinnamon, salt and flour in a separate bowl. Combine the wet and dry mixtures. Dissolve the baking soda in the buttermilk; pour into the dough. Add the raisins. Work the extra sugar into each ball before rolling to make a crisper cookie. Roll the dough out and cut into squares. Sprinkle the extra sugar on the tops of each cookie before baking. Bake at 350 degrees for 12 minutes or until lightly brown.

Desserts

CONVERSATION STOPPERS

Chocolate Chip Cheesecake

**32-ounce package chocolate chip cookie dough
Two 8-ounce packages cream cheese, softened
1/3 cup sugar
1 tablespoon vanilla extract**

Slice the cookie dough; pat the slices into the bottom of a coated 9 x 13-inch baking dish. Combine the cream cheese, sugar and vanilla extract until creamy and smooth. Pat the remaining slices of the dough in hands; place on the top covering the entire dish. Bake at 400 degrees covered for 15 minutes. Uncover and bake an additional 15 minutes. Let cool.

Serves 20

*T*his is one of the most popular recipes I make. Everyone always wants a copy of it when I serve it and they can't believe how easy it is to make. I have varied the recipe by using other refrigerated cookie dough—chocolate dough with white chocolate, chocolate chunks, and white chocolate chips with macadamia nuts. My favorite, however, will always be the chocolate chip.

Oreo Cheesecake

4 cups crushed Oreo cookies
5 tablespoons butter, melted
Three 8-ounce packages cream cheese,
at room temperature
I cup sugar
5 large eggs, at room temperature

Combine 2 cups of the Oreo crumbs and melted butter; mix well. Press the mixture into a 9-inch springform pan. Combine the cream cheese, sugar and eggs; beat using an electric mixer at medium speed until smooth and fluffy. Stir in the remaining Oreo crumbs. Bake at 300 degrees, covered with aluminum foil, for 25 minutes. Remove the aluminum foil and cook for an additional 25 minutes. Turn off the oven, leave the oven door ajar and allow the cake to cool for 20 minutes. Remove the cake from the oven and place on a wire rack. Cover and refrigerate for 2 hours after the cake is completely cool. Uncover the cheesecake and remove from the pan when ready to serve.

Serves 10

This was my first cheesecake recipe. It took me many cracked cakes before I got it right. Sometimes my cakes still crack a bit and I either crush more Oreos and sprinkle them over the top or I slice the cake and place it on plates with a swirl of chocolate syrup over the top. Crack or no crack this cheesecake is rich and delicious.

RICH IN FLAVOR

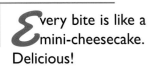very bite is like a
mini-cheesecake.
Delicious!

Chocolate Chip Cheese Ball

8 ounces cream cheese, softened
2 sticks butter
3/4 cup confectioners' sugar
2 tablespoons brown sugar
1/2 teaspoon vanilla extract
3/4 cup milk chocolate chips
3/4 cup chopped pecans

Combine the cream cheese, butter, sugars, vanilla extract
and chocolate chips. Chill until firm. Roll the mixture into
a ball; roll in the pecans. Serve with graham crackers.

Serves 20

Yummy Bars

18.25-ounce box white cake mix
1 stick butter
3 eggs, divided
1 cup chopped pecans
3 teaspoons vanilla extract, divided
8 ounces cream cheese
16 ounces confectioners' sugar

Combine the cake mix, butter, 1 of the eggs, pecans and 1 1/2 teaspoon of the vanilla extract; press in the bottom of a coated 9 x 13-inch baking dish. Combine the cream cheese, the remaining eggs, confectioners' sugar and the remaining vanilla extract. Pour over the crust. Bake at 350 degrees for 40 to 45 minutes. Cut into squares.

Variations: For a treat in the fall use a spice cake mix, almond extract instead of vanilla and sprinkle almonds on top. Change the cake mix to chocolate and sprinkle chocolate chips on top or use a lemon cake mix and substitute lemon extract for vanilla. The great thing about this recipe is that you can be creative using just about any cake mix and flavoring combination.

Toffee Bars

1 1/2 sleeves saltine crackers, crushed
2 sticks butter
1 cup brown sugar
12 ounces semisweet chocolate chips

Line a coated jelly roll pan with the saltine cracker crumbs. Combine the butter and brown sugar; boil for 3 minutes. Spread the mixture over the crackers. Bake at 425 degrees for 3 minutes. Sprinkle the chocolate chips over the top; let stand for 5 minutes. Spread the chocolate; refrigerate until cool. Go around the edge of the pan using a knife and flip out using a spatula; break into pieces.

Easy Fruit Cobbler

1 stick butter
2 cup sugar, divided
1 cup all-purpose flour
1 1/2 teaspoons baking powder
3/4 cup milk
2 cups fresh fruit: blackberries, blueberries, cherries, or peaches

Preheat the oven to 350 degrees. Place the butter in a 9 x 13-inch glass baking dish; put in the oven to melt. Blend 1 cup of the sugar, flour, baking powder and milk. Pour the sugar mixture over the melted butter. Cover with the fruit. Sprinkle the remaining sugar on top. Bake for 30 minutes.

Serves 10

Nancy's Banana Pudding

Two 3-ounce packages of vanilla instant pudding
14-ounce can sweetened condensed milk
11-ounce box vanilla wafers
6 bananas, sliced
8-ounce container whipped topping

Prepare the pudding according to package directions. Add the sweetened condensed milk. Layer the vanilla wafers, bananas, pudding mixture and whipped topping; repeat. Refrigerate until serving.

*N*ancy says you can substitute sugar-free instant pudding, skim milk and reduced-fat sweetened condensed milk to experience less guilt for your waistline.

Old-Fashioned Bread Pudding

1/2 stick butter, melted
8 slices French bread, torn into small pieces
4 cups milk
1 1/2 cups sugar
4 eggs
1/3 cup golden raisins
1/4 teaspoon salt
Bourbon Sauce

Pour the butter into an 8 x 12 x 2-inch baking dish. Place the pieces of bread in a large mixing bowl. Add the milk and soak for 5 minutes. Combine the sugar, eggs, raisins and salt. Add to the bread; mix well. Pour into the baking dish and bake at 350 degrees for 1 hour. Serve topped with Bourbon Sauce.

Bourbon Sauce

1/2 cup butter
1 cup sugar
1/4 cup water
1 egg, beaten
1/3 cup bourbon

Melt the butter in a small saucepan over a medium heat. Add the sugar and water; cook, stirring for 1 minute. Gradually add the butter and sugar to the egg, beating constantly. Slowly stir in the bourbon.

Makes 6 servings

Party Pumpkin Roll

3 eggs
1 cup sugar
2/3 cup canned pumpkin
1 teaspoon lemon juice
3/4 cup all-purpose flour
1 teaspoon baking powder
2 teaspoons cinnamon
1 teaspoon ginger
1/2 teaspoon nutmeg
1/2 teaspoon salt
1 cup finely-chopped pecans
1 1/4 cups confectioners' sugar, divided
3 ounces cream cheese, softened
4 tablespoons butter
1/2 teaspoon vanilla extract

Beat the eggs for 5 minutes using an electric mixer on high speed. Add the sugar gradually. Stir in the pumpkin and lemon juice. Combine the flour, baking powder, cinnamon, ginger, nutmeg and salt in a separate bowl. Fold the dry ingredients into the pumpkin mixture. Spread the mixture on a coated jelly roll pan. Sprinkle the chopped pecans on top. Bake at 350 degrees for 15 minutes. Turn the cake out on top of a thin towel sprinkled with 1/4 cup of the confectioners' sugar; let cool. Combine the remaining confectioners' sugar, cream cheese, butter and vanilla extract. Spread on the top of the cooled cake. Roll tightly using the towel starting at the short side of the cake. Refrigerate for 2 hours; slice and serve.

Southern Supreme Brownies

If I ever take these brownies to a church function, I leave the nuts out since many people are allergic to nuts and it still tastes great.

18.25-ounce box German chocolate cake mix
2/3 cup evaporated milk, divided
3/4 cup melted butter
1 cup semisweet chocolate chips
1 cup chopped pecans
14-ounce package caramels, unwrapped

Combine the cake mix, 1/3 cup of the evaporated milk and butter. Spread 1/2 of the mixture into a coated 9 x 13-inch baking dish. Bake at 350 degrees for 15 minutes. Remove from the oven and top with the chocolate chips and pecans. Melt the caramels and 1/3 cup of the evaporated milk in a bowl in the microwave or in a small saucepan; stir until smooth. Drizzle the caramel mixture on top of the baked cake layer. Drop the remaining cake mixture by small spoonfuls evenly over the caramel. Bake an additional 15 minutes or until firm.

Serves 20

Chocolate Fondue

14-ounce can sweetened condensed milk
7-ounce jar marshmallow creme
12-ounce package semisweet chocolate chips
2 tablespoons crunchy peanut butter
1/4 cup milk

Combine the sweetened condensed milk, marshmallow creme, chocolate chips and peanut butter in a saucepan. Cook over a medium heat; stir constantly. Add the milk slowly when melted. Serve with fruit or angel food cake.

Hello Dolly Pie

1/2 cup semisweet chocolate chips
1/2 cup butterscotch chips
1/2 cup shredded coconut
1/2 cup chopped pecans
9-inch graham cracker piecrust
14-ounce can sweetened condensed milk

Pour the chips, coconut and pecans into the piecrust. Pour the sweetened condensed milk over the top. Bake at 350 degrees for 30 minutes or until brown. Cool before serving.

"M&M's" Pie

I serve this often because it is so easy and I get such a great response from it. It is very rich, so one pie goes a long way.

1 stick butter, softened
1/2 cup all-purpose flour
1 cup sugar
1/2 cup "M&M's" Plain Chocolate Candies
1 teaspoon vanilla extract
2 eggs, beaten
9-inch piecrust, unbaked

Combine the butter, flour, sugar, "M&M's", vanilla extract and eggs. Fold into the piecrust. Bake, uncovered, at 375 degrees for 20 to 25 minutes or until the top is golden brown.

Serves 8

The Best Peach Pie

This is my mother's recipe and I think it is the easiest and best peach pie around!

1 egg
1/3 cup melted butter
1/3 cup self-rising flour
1 cup sugar
1 teaspoon vanilla extract
3 to 4 fresh peaches, peeled and sliced
9-inch piecrust, unbaked

Combine the egg, butter, flour, sugar and vanilla extract. Place the sliced peaches in the bottom of the piecrust. Pour the mixture over the peaches. Bake at 350 degrees for 1 hour or until brown.

Bama Blueberry Pie

3/4 cup sugar
2 1/2 tablespoons cornstarch
1/4 teaspoon salt
2/3 cup water
3 cups blueberries, divided
2 tablespoons butter
1 1/2 tablespoons lemon juice
9-inch piecrust, baked

Combine the sugar, cornstarch, salt, water and 1 cup of the blueberries in a saucepan. Bring the mixture to a boil and cook until thick. Stir in the butter and lemon juice. Cool to room temperature and fold in the remaining blueberries. Pour into the piecrust and chill for at least 2 hours.

Hershey Bar Pie

1 1/3 cups coconut
1/2 stick butter, melted
Six 1.55-ounce Hersheys candy bars with almonds
1 teaspoon instant coffee granules
16-ounce container whipped topping

Place the coconut into a 9-inch pie plate. Pour the butter over the coconut. Press the coconut down with a fork until it is mashed together to look like a crust. Bake at 300 degrees for 8 minutes. Melt the candy bars in a saucepan. Add the coffee and whipped topping; mix well and fold into the pie shell. Refrigerate for 2 hours.

Lemon Icebox Pie

14-ounce can sweetened condensed milk
12-ounce can frozen lemonade concentrate, thawed
16-ounce container whipped topping
2 graham cracker piecrusts

Combine the sweetened condensed milk, lemonade and whipped topping. Place in the graham cracker piecrusts and freeze for 2 hours.

Makes 2 pies

Mamaw's Strawberry Cake

Each Christmas morning, our family has a Birthday Party for Jesus. My little girls enjoy celebrating with this cake. It is moist and very sweet.

18.25 ounce box white cake mix
4 eggs, beaten
1 cup oil
3-ounce box strawberry gelatin
1/2 cup frozen strawberries, thawed, reserving juice
1-pound package confectioners' sugar
1 stick butter

Combine the cake mix, eggs and oil. Combine the gelatin with 1/2 cup boiling water; let cool. Fold the strawberries into the gelatin. Pour the gelatin mixture into the cake mixture; blend well. Pour the batter into a coated 9 x 13-inch cake pan or two 9-inch round cake pans. Bake at 350 degrees until a wooden pick removes clean. Combine the confectioners' sugar, butter and strawberry juice until smooth for frosting.

Yellow Velvet Cake

18.25-ounce box lemon cake mix
3-ounce box lemon instant pudding
1/4 cup oil
1/4 cup water
4 eggs, beaten
1/2 cup lemon juice
2 tablespoons butter
2 cups confectioners' sugar

Combine the cake mix, pudding, oil, water and eggs in a large mixing bowl; blend well. Pour the batter into a coated 10-inch tube pan. Bake at 325 degrees for 45 to 50 minutes. Remove the cake from the oven and leave in the pan. Poke holes all over the top of the cake with a fork. Combine the lemon juice, butter and confectioners' sugar in a saucepan; bring to a boil. Pour the hot sauce over the cake. Let the cake cool completely before removing from the pan. Turn the cake out of the pan; dust the top of the cake with confectioners' sugar.

Serves 10

Chocolate Lover's Favorite Cake

18.25-ounce box butter cake mix
Two 3-ounce boxes chocolate instant pudding
4 eggs, beaten
1 1/2 cups water
1 1/2 cups oil
6 ounces semisweet chocolate chips
16.50-ounce can chocolate fudge frosting

Combine the cake mix, pudding, eggs, water and oil using an electric mixer. Add the chocolate chips. Pour the batter into a coated bundt pan. Bake at 350 degrees for 1 hour. Cool completely and remove from the pan. Melt the can of frosting in the microwave and drizzle over the top of the cake.

Easy Apple Cake with Cream Topping

20-ounce can apple fruit filling
2 cups all-purpose flour
1 cup sugar
1 1/2 teaspoons baking soda
1 teaspoon salt
2 eggs, beaten
1 teaspoon vanilla extract
2/3 cup oil
3/4 cup chopped walnuts, divided

Spread the apple fruit filling over the bottom of a coated 9 x 13-inch baking dish. Combine the flour, sugar, baking soda and salt; sprinkle over the fruit filling. Blend the eggs, vanilla extract, oil and 1/2 cup of the walnuts; pour over the flour mixture. Stir with a fork only until blended, smoothing the batter evenly. Bake at 350 degrees for 40 to 50 minutes or until the cake springs back when lightly touched. Pour hot Cream Topping over the warm cake; sprinkle with remaining walnuts. Serve warm or cold.

Cream Topping

1 cup sugar
1/2 cup sour cream
1/2 teaspoon baking soda

Combine the sugar, sour cream and baking soda in a saucepan; cook over a medium heat. Stir constantly until it boils. Pour over cake.

Julie's Fabulous Chocolate Chip Pound Cake

Southern hospitality is at its best upon the birth of a baby. When my son, Joby, was born we received so many wonderful meals. My friend Julie always makes this cake for new moms and it truly makes those middle of the night feedings a happy time!

18.25 ounce box butter cake mix
3.4-ounce package vanilla instant pudding
4 eggs, beaten
1/2 cup oil
1/2 cup water
8 ounces sour cream
1 1/2 cups semisweet chocolate chips, divided
1 cup brown sugar

Combine the cake mix, pudding, eggs, oil, water and sour cream. Pour 1/3 of the batter into a coated bundt pan. Sprinkle 3/4 cup of the chocolate chips on top. Sprinkle 1/2 cup of the light brown sugar on top. Add the remaining batter and sprinkle with the remaining chocolate chips and light brown sugar. Bake at 350 degrees for 25 minutes, uncovered. Cover with aluminum foil and bake an additional 20 minutes. Cool for 15 to 20 minutes before removing from the pan. Place on a platter with the chocolate chip and brown sugar side up.

Coconut Cake

18.25-ounce box butter cake mix
2 cups sugar
1 cup sour cream
12 ounces frozen coconut, thawed
1 1/2 cups whipped cream

Prepare the cake according to the package direction; pour in two coated 9-inch cake pans. Cut each layer in half making 4 layers. Combine the sugar, sour cream and coconut; chill. Blend 1/3 of the coconut mixture with the whipped cream. Ice between the layers with the remaining coconut mixture. Ice the top of the cake using the whipped cream mixture. Best made 3 days ahead.

Hot Fudge-Style Crock Pot Cake

1 3/4 cups brown sugar, divided
1 cup all-purpose flour
1/4 cup plus 3 tablespoons unsweetened cocoa, divided
2 teaspoons baking powder
1/2 teaspoon salt
1/2 cup milk
2 tablespoons butter, melted
1/2 teaspoon vanilla extract
1 3/4 cups boiling water

Combine 1 cup of the brown sugar, flour, 3 tablespoons of the cocoa, baking powder and salt in a bowl. Stir in the milk, butter and vanilla extract. Spread the mixture over the bottom of a 3 1/2- quart slow cooker. Combine the remaining brown sugar and cocoa in a separate bowl; sprinkle evenly over the mixture in the slow cooker; do not stir. Pour in the boiling water. Do not stir. Cover; cook on high for 2 to 3 hours or until a wooden pick inserted comes out clean. Serve warm with ice cream or whipped topping.

Serves 6 to 8

This dessert is only complete with Homemade Chocolate Sauce.

Homemade Chocolate Sauce

12-ounce package semisweet chocolate chips
1-pound package confectioners' sugar
12-ounce can evaporated milk
1 stick butter

Melt the chocolate in the top of a double boiler or microwave. Add the confectioners' sugar, evaporated milk and butter; mix well. Boil for 4 to 5 minutes. Place in a sterilized jar. Keep refrigerated and reheat when needed.

Piña Colada Cake

18.25-ounce box yellow cake mix
6 ounces frozen coconut, thawed and divided
20-ounce can crushed pineapple,
drained, reserving juice
14-ounce can sweetened condensed milk
15-ounce can cream of coconut
16 ounces whipped topping

This makes a very moist cake!

Prepare the cake mix according to the package directions adding 3 ounces of the coconut and substituting the pineapple juice for liquid in recipe. Bake in a greased 9 x 13-inch baking dish. Poke holes in the top of the cake after removing it from the oven. Combine the sweetened condensed milk and cream of coconut; pour over the cake. Combine the crushed pineapple and whipped topping. Spread over the cake and sprinkle with the remaining coconut.

Simple Chocolate Tort

18.25-ounce box chocolate cake mix
3 cups heavy cream
I cup crushed almonds or pecans

Prepare the cake mix according to the package directions. Place the batter in three coated 9-inch baking pans. Cut each layer in half using a small thread. Beat the cream until whipped. Pour over each layer and the top of the cake. Garnish with the nuts.

Lemon Tart

9-inch refrigerated piecrust
2 cups sugar
1/2 cup butter, softened
5 eggs, beaten
I cup milk
I tablespoon all-purpose flour
I tablespoon cornmeal
1/4 cup fresh lemon juice
2 tablespoons lemon zest

Mold the piecrust into a pie plate. Combine the sugar and butter; cream using an electric mixer until light and fluffy. Beat in the eggs and milk. Add the flour, cornmeal, lemon juice and lemon zest; blend until smooth. Pour the mixture into the piecrust. Bake at 350 degrees for 35 to 40 minutes or until done.

Tailgating

GAME DAY GOURMET

Dilly Oyster Crackers

This is a nice snack to put out for casual get-togethers. I like to make a large batch and place in an air-tight container to use when needed.

1-ounce package ranch dressing mix
1 tablespoon dillweed
1/2 teaspoon garlic powder
1/2 cup vegetable oil
16-ounce box oyster crackers

Combine the dressing mix, dillweed, garlic powder and vegetable oil. Marinate the oyster crackers overnight. Bake at 350 degrees for 1 hour.

Richard's Bean Soup

Three 14-ounce cans Great Northern beans
1 cup chopped carrots
1 cup chopped celery
1 onion, chopped
1 cup sliced mushrooms
1 pound Polish sausage, cut into bite-size pieces
1 stick butter
Two 5.5-ounce cans vegetable juice
2 teaspoons salt
1 teaspoon pepper

Place the beans in a stock pot adding three cans of water. Sauté the carrots, celery, onion, mushrooms and Polish sausage in butter in a skillet; add to the beans. Add the vegetable juice. Season with the salt and pepper. Simmer for 1 hour.

Serves 12

Beer Chili

1 1/2 pounds ground beef
1 onion, chopped
1 green pepper, chopped
1 garlic clove, minced
6 slices bacon, cooked and crumbled
10-ounce can tomato soup
12-ounce can beer
10 ounces tomato sauce
Two 15-ounce cans kidney beans
3 tablespoons chili powder
1 1/2 teaspoons salt
1/2 teaspoon cumin
1/4 teaspoon ground cloves
2 teaspoons Accent
1 teaspoon Mrs. Dash
1 teaspoon Tabasco sauce

I love all chili but this is my favorite. The beer gives it a different flavor and the bacon is an added treat! This chili will really warm you up—it has quite a kick to it!

Brown the ground beef; drain. Add the onion and pepper; sauté adding the garlic at the last minute. Add the bacon, tomato soup, beer, tomato sauce, beans, chili powder, salt, cumin, cloves, Accent, Mrs. Dash and Tabasco sauce. Simmer for 2 hours, adding more beer if the consistency is too thick.

Serves 6

For a more tame chili, omit the Tabasco sauce and cut the chili powder down to 2 tablespoons.

Date Bars

16 ounces chopped dates
1 cup water
2 teaspoons vanilla extract
4 cups rolled oats
3 cups all-purpose flour
1 1/2 teaspoons baking soda
1 1/2 teaspoons salt
1 1/2 cups butter, melted
1/2 cup maple syrup

Purée the dates, water and vanilla extract. Combine the oats, flour, baking soda, salt, butter and maple syrup. Pour 1/2 of the oatmeal mixture in the bottom of a coated 9 x 13-inch baking dish. Pour the date mixture over the top. Add the rest of the oatmeal mixture on top. Bake at 350 degrees for 15 minutes.

Serves 20

Sandwich for the Crowd

2 loaves unsliced Italian bread
8 ounces cream cheese, softened
I cup shredded Cheddar cheese
3/4 cup chopped green onion
1/4 cup mayonnaise
1/2 tablespoon Worcestershire sauce
I pound ham, thinly sliced
I pound turkey or roast beef, thinly sliced
12 to 14 dill pickle slices

Cut the loaves in half lengthwise. Hollow out the top and bottom leaving a 1/2-inch shell. Combine the cheeses, onion, mayonnaise and Worcestershire sauce. Spread over the bread shells. Layer the meats on the top halves and the pickles on the bottom halves. Gently press the two halves together. Wrap in plastic and refrigerate for at least two hours. Cut into I 1/2-inch slices.

Ham and Cabbage Salad

1 head cabbage, uncooked
4 to 5 green onions, chopped
1 cup red grapes, sliced in half
1/2 cup toasted almonds, sliced
2 cups cooked ham, cubed
6 tablespoons apple cider vinegar
4 tablespoons sugar
1 cup vegetable oil
1 teaspoon salt
2 3-ounce packages chicken-flavored ramen noodles,
crushed, reserving seasoning packets

Shred the cabbage into bite-size pieces. Add the onions; mix well. Add the grapes, almonds and ham; chill until serving. Combine the vinegar, sugar, oil, salt and ramen noodle seasoning; shake and chill. Pour the dressing over the cabbage salad immediately before serving. Top with crushed ramen noodles.

Hearty Beans

1 pound dry pinto beans,
soaked in water overnight
1/4 pound bacon, diced
3 onions, diced and divided
4 teaspoons salt, divided
1 1/2 teaspoons garlic salt, divided
1 teaspoon pepper, divided
2 green peppers, diced
2 pounds ground beef
1 teaspoon cumin
1 teaspoon oregano
1/2 teaspoon tarragon
1 teaspoon Worcestershire sauce
28-ounce can diced tomatoes
6-ounce can tomato paste
8 ounces ketchup

Boil the beans, bacon, 1 of the onions, 2 teaspoons of the salt, 1/2 teaspoon of the garlic salt and 1/2 teaspoon of the pepper for two hours. Sauté the remaining onion and green peppers. Add the ground beef and brown. Add the remaining garlic salt, salt, pepper, cumin, oregano, tarragon, Worcestershire sauce, tomatoes, tomato paste and ketchup. Simmer for one hour; add the beans and simmer for an additional hour.

Ballgame Brisket

4-ounce bottle liquid smoke
15-ounce bottle Heinz 57 Steak Sauce
2 cups water
1 1/2 tablespoons Worcestershire sauce
1/4 teaspoon hot sauce
4 pound brisket
1 1/2 tablespoons garlic salt
1/4 cup brown sugar

Combine the liquid smoke, Heinz 57 Steak Sauce, water, Worcestershire sauce and hot sauce. Sprinkle the meat generously with the garlic salt. Place the meat in a large baking pan; pour the liquid smoke over the meat. Cover tightly with aluminum foil. Bake at 250 degrees for 5 hours; uncovering during the last hour. Slice the meat thinly and place in the sauce. Add the brown sugar.

Linda Batchelor's White Sauce

Great on brisket but even better on chicken!

1 cup mayonnaise
1 tablespoon salt
1 tablespoon pepper
2 tablespoons sugar
3 tablespoons vinegar
4 tablespoons lemon juice

Combine all of the ingredients in an airtight container; shake vigorously.

Serves 8

Index